I0567306

Mind Control

Unlock Your Full Potential Stop
Procrastination and Leave Your
Failures in the Past

*(Learn the Dark Secrets of Hypnosis Manipulation
Deception and Human Psychology)*

Mathew King

Published By **Oliver Leish**

Mathew King

Mind Control: Unlock Your Full Potential Stop Procrastination and Leave Your Failures in the Past (Learn the Dark Secrets of Hypnosis Manipulation Deception and Human Psychology)

ISBN   978-1-998769-95-7

No part of this guidebook shall be reproduced in any form without permission in writing from the publisher except in the case of brief quotations embodied in critical articles or reviews.

Legal & Disclaimer

The information contained in this ebook is not designed to replace or take the place of any form of medicine or professional medical advice. The information in this ebook has been provided for educational & entertainment purposes only.

The information contained in this book has been compiled from sources deemed reliable, and it is accurate to the best of the Author's knowledge; however, the Author cannot guarantee its accuracy and validity and cannot be held liable for any errors or omissions. Changes are periodically made to this book. You must consult your doctor or get professional medical advice before using any of the suggested remedies, techniques, or information in this book.

Table Of Contents

Chapter 1: The Concept Of Mind Control

Most human beings recall that mind control, otherwise known as brainwashing, perception reform, or concept control, has been spherical whilst you do not forget that information commenced. While this could be rather genuine, it's only in recent times that it has come to be a popular place of test and studies.

People have been engaged in manipulation as a way of social and sexual control, political gamesmanship and revenge, for eons. Think about King David. He appeared out at some degree inside the town one morning and observed Bathsheba taking a bath on a neighboring rooftop. It wasn't prolonged earlier than he were given her husband suitable and under the influence of alcohol and despatched him off to the the the front of a raging conflict from which he in no way again. David preferred Bathsheba. Her husband became within the manner and so, in immoderate manipulative style, he eliminated the roadblock!

And how about the ones Borgias and their manipulator in chief, Machiavelli? They were masters of the game. They now not only neutralized their enemies, the Orsinis, but made them journey to the scene of the crime on their own steam, believing that peace had miraculously been made.

Machiavelli famously stated, "No agency is more likely to achieve success than one concealed from the enemy till it is ripe for execution." And that enemy must be saved close to! A hold close baby-kisser, Machiavelli end up the exemplar of the manipulative thoughts, continuously one step earlier of oldsters that would bring about the autumn of the princely Borgias.

But manipulative mind manage and brainwashing are amazing animals. Brainwashing is a noticeably new issue and lots centered at the violent and coercive compliance of the subjects it's practiced on.

It was at a few degree inside the Korean War that the term brainwashing modified into coined and delivered to the dictionary. Unfortunately, on the equal time because it changed into added, it emerge as given a terrible connotation, due to the truth while the Korean War application changed into simply malevolent, brainwashing can in reality be used for appropriate (greater on that in a minute).

The word end up used to provide an reason for why 21 some of the 20,000 American prisoners of war (POW) defected to their communist enemies. There modified into additionally an incident wherein a few POW's were recommended to confess to having waged natural war (which that they'd, in fact, no longer done).
There is, however, a high-quality difference amongst thoughts control and brainwashing this isn't frequently made. Most humans frequently use the ones phrases for 2 very unique mind interchangeably, however how they art work is highly distinctive, one from the alternative, as you will see showed below. After studying the reasons provided, you can see they are absolutely extraordinary and that one in every of them does not constitute the same type of manipulation (or deception) this is useful in your ordinary lifestyles.

No matter range the way you word it, having a person compel you to make a dramatic trade for your existence, based on their private will, is not a top notch. The most vital part of this ebook is centered on coaching you the manner

3

to recognize in case you are being manipulated, managed or brainwashed with the resource of others. You will learn how to apprehend the symptoms and signs and a way to combat decrease back at the same time as someone attempts to manipulate your thoughts as a way to have an effect to your life in a horrible way.

Brainwashing

Basically, what makes brainwashing extraordinary from manipulation is the device gone thru with the useful resource of the issue in question. In brainwashing, the man or woman is aware that the manipulators (or sellers) are enemies, and that he is being driven within the course of a nice conduct or attitude beneath the manage of these humans. In order to save you the possibility of bodily pressure or violence being inflicted on him, submission to the imposed perception device is the opportunity often (if no longer generally) decided on. Should the brainwashing technique be discontinued, the sufferer will every now and then either absolutely or in component get better and regain his precise individuality and powers of independent notion.

Some humans but, by no means regain the college of questioning for themselves. They stay brainwashed. If you watched returned to sports that transpired in Waco, Texas underneath cult chief, David Koresh, you may recognize. These humans have been brainwashed into believing the exceptional manner they might gain the everlasting bliss promised with the useful resource of Koresh changed into to test the schooling of a person who've end up absolutely insane. As with cult predecessor, Jim Jones, the leader of a cult in Guyana that devoted mass suicide thru eating poisoned Kool-Aid (the foundation of the announcing "don't drink the Kool-Aid"), Koresh brainwashed his enthusiasts into unquestioning belief in each word he stated. We'll communicate the have an impact on of cults and the way they indoctrinate human beings into unwavering perception in extra detail, later in this e-book.

People subjected to prolonged brainwashing, bolstered for years (just like the ones in the cult examples above) regularly don't get better. While a few get better after acknowledging they feigned elegance of the brainwashing as a coping mechanism, others in no manner regain their powers of independent belief. This is why you could not be analyzing a way to brainwash others within the pages of this e-book. I will no longer educate you a way to brainwash human beings. I will, but, educate you the manner to control and steer humans's minds for your personal gain. I will no longer teach you the manner to do this in a malicious way and that's precisely what brainwashing is - a malicious shape of thoughts manage.

Throughout records, humans have used manipulation as a manner to get huge corporations of humans, or possibly a unmarried individual, to comply with their non-public idea manner and schedule. Typically, this ends negatively. Brainwashing is frequently used by cults and similar agencies of human beings to control the minds of massive numbers of humans, as we've referred to above, with the examples of David Koresh and Jim Jones.

Malicious thoughts manipulate can also occur in situations like romantic relationships wherein one character wants to govern the thoughts and movements of the alternative person. No depend the manner you put it, or what scenario you placed it in, brainwashing is in no manner appropriate!

Mind Control
The method of mind manage, instead, is infinitely subtler and the effect, more long term

or maybe (at times) unfavorable. In this approach, the manipulator enters the individual's existence as a pal or teacher - an person nicely well worth trusting and believing in. From the very beginning, the sufferer of the manipulator may additionally furthermore have already allow all defenses down and may even willingly take part in the mind manage way. There can be no physical pressure concerned in any way, and the victim can also moreover additionally be below the misconception that he is making all choices with the aid of himself.

Mind control desires to change someone to the very center with the beneficial useful resource of changing their choices, notion, ideals, values, behaviors and relationships. The technique is diffused and sluggish. Often, the sufferer is unaware of how big the manipulation is, if now not actually oblivious to it. The manipulation will, but, comprise social and highbrow strain and force, whether or not or not the reason is privy to those effects or now not.

Because sufferers of mind manipulate are beneath the effect that the choice to undertake new values and beliefs has been made via them, and the fact that the agent is appeared as a relied on friend, although the manipulation is discontinued, the new identity that has been long-mounted by way of thru have an impact on will hold to persist. In essence, whilst people count on the modifications they have got embraced are impartial resolutions, they may be much more likely to passively accept and even warfare to preserve them. This is what makes thoughts manage fairly dangerous, if used for the wrong motives and with malicious rationale. Its effects are extra powerful than brainwashing and it it's a long time project that may certainly disable and scar the victim.

It is also essential to be aware that even though mind control is particularly unethical, it can be used for correctly reason. People laid low with addiction troubles can be subjected to this process to treatment them in their dependancy. However, you have to additionally be conscious that human beings can use this device on you and that folks who are at risk of it could bear in mind that they'll be following their personal instincts, whilst they may be, in reality, following the diffused direction of the controller.

Now which you recognize thoughts manipulate is feasible, are you able to determined of all and sundry who has tried mind manage on you? You might not comprehend it, however as you have been growing up, your mother and father used a shape of mind manage to shape you into the character you are in recent times. They massaged you proper right into a shape society deems normal and appropriate with the useful resource of the use of subtly steerage you within the route of positive behaviors, beliefs and values. You can also be aware that a number of the alternatives on your regular lifestyles are because of thoughts manage. Don't accept as true with me? Look at your every day ordinary.

Your mother and father used mind manipulate to train you to get up, bathe, brush your tooth, dress, in all likelihood do your makeup, brush your hair, and appearance presentable earlier than you left the residence. This is a form of top notch mind manage. They additionally taught you which you need to have an annual check-up on the physician, see your dentist often and keep a wholesome diet regime. See, thoughts control does not constantly want to be a awful strain for your lifestyles. It can with out difficulty purpose satisfactory results.

Extent of Effectiveness

Mind manage is possible to reverse. Its outcomes want no longer be eternal. However, this could depend carefully on how enormous the manipulation has been, or how deep the relationship of the victim is to the agent of the mind control that's been practiced. Some special elements that might have an impact on mind control are enumerated beneath:

The wide type of techniques performed at the sufferer. ☐

➢ Duration of exposure to manipulation, how long in step with consultation and the manner frequently.
➢ How deep the relationship of the sufferer is collectively along with his own family and friends, and what sort of interplay and help he gets from them.
➢ Whether the sufferer is permitted to have outdoor publicity and for a manner lengthy.
➢ If sexual abuse and hypnosis is implemented.
➢ How a whole lot direct contact the victim has with the agent.

All of those may also moreover sound darkish and horrid, but it is vital to phrase that every one of those can take place within the maximum harmless-looking setting, like seminars, camps, and wonderful similar sports activities. Even meeting a modern day friend and getting too intimate in too quick a time may moreover furthermore motive mind control. Romantic relationships are often based totally totally on thoughts manipulate, to a point. You also can agree with that every one your hobbies are really yours, even though you can find out at a future date, at the same time as the relationship is no longer a legitimate one, that they have been in fact the pastimes of your associate. Being more potent than you mentally, it's even possible that your accomplice became aware of controlling you and your possibilities, to alternate the manner you perceived the area you shared with him.

Relationships are a outstanding example of mind manipulate. This is because of the fact some people use thoughts manage to draw functionality pals. Pretending to be a certain way certainly prolonged sufficient to attract inside the person they expect they need to spend their lives with, they may be able to alternate without warning after only a short time frame. Having led the mate, they've fooled into believing they're a person they're no longer, the agent of mind manage will show himself and the relationship will implode.

Example of a Bad Relationship
A brilliant instance of a awful courting is one that nowadays made the records. A girl modified into married for six years to what she concept emerge as "the person of her goals." She stayed with him thru a sequence of horrible activities, believing she loved him. She allowed his own family to move in with them. She suffered bodily and intellectual abuse from her accomplice and his circle of relatives, and persisted sexual abuse from her companion for years.

During the time she end up together with her associate, she did no longer understand that each time she made a chum in the neighborhood, he decided that they had been shifting. She modified into now not allowed to go shopping by myself, or maybe to have cash of her non-public. Even though she had a activity, she needed to hand her paycheck over to her accomplice every payday.

This story ended better than maximum. After six years of abuse, she located out what became taking location and that she changed into a hostage in her very own domestic. She determined out that she changed into being held over again from living a entire, glad life and that she turn out to be being controlled. She packed her things, and taking her kids, left for real.

In an attempt to get out of the relationship, she decided that moving become the great opportunity. When she reached the door with the last of her gadgets, and the two children in tow, she emerge as met at the door via way of her partner, wielding a sword. The concept of losing manipulate of her end up too much for this manipulative control freak to bear.

The moral of the story is that this man turn out to be now not mainly worried with the truth he grow to be losing his female friend, or his kids. What he become worried with losing turn out to be six years' hard, manipulative, mind-controlling paintings. He had manipulated, abused and managed this feminine for goodbye, he didn't recognize a few other manner to live. The fact is, neither did she. It took her five years to discover ways to stay a brand new and regular life; one which did no longer comprise abuse, forget, thoughts manage, or being continuously uprooted as a way of controlling her.

When someone is in a courting like this, it is able to take years to alter to growing their non-public picks and may in the end cause remedy at the way to paintings via the issues and the damage that has been due to mind manage and abuse. Many sufferers pop out of relationships like this saying that the physical abuse turned into now not anything in assessment to the mental abuse they suffered in the state of affairs. Bruises fade, and so does the ache. Emotional abuse, alternatively, leaves a long lasting have an impact on that could exchange someone for the relaxation in their lives. It can permanently damage someone to the aspect in which they don't apprehend a manner to live independently, or with out the regularity and familiarity of the abuse they've got escaped.

Who Uses Mind Control?
Cults are universally seemed to make use of thoughts control to facilitate the complete obedience of their fans. This isn't always constrained to agencies sporting white coats and mask, or folks that shave their heads to differentiate themselves. Even the smoothest-speakme man in a graceful healthy ought to

have the aim of manipulation. Even the awesome looking woman with a normal day challenge can be a member of a cult. These organizations have end up so sophisticated that, even though we're all acquainted with them and the manner they perform, many nonetheless fall prey to their guarantees and manipulation. Below is a listing of organizations, sectors, establishments and professions stated to apply the manner of mind control:

➤ Religions
➤ Politics
➤ Philosophy
➤ Science
➤ Sports
➤ Meditation
➤ Healing recuperation methods
➤ Personal Development
➤ Money Making (E.G. Community advertising and marketing, and stock trade)
➤ Psychology
➤ Plastic Surgery
➤ Western medication
➤ Mass media
➤ Education

And the list is going on as lots as, extensively, such regions as hairdressing. Because manipulation isn't approximately which organisation or corporation or profession human beings are located in. It's approximately human beings and the human nature absolutely everyone share.

Basically, all and sundry can fall victim to a cult, and the mind manipulate they hire without identifying it. The high-quality element all people can desire for is that there is no purpose for the manipulator to take benefit of the sufferer. Also, that they're capable of decide they're being manipulated in advance than promoting all their assets and giving the proceeds to the cult, or worse, consuming the Kool-Aid!

It is vital to test that agencies, businesses, and professions aren't the only areas in which thoughts manipulate is employed. Random human beings can use thoughts control on anyone, and, frequently, with malicious purpose. Some serial killers and psychopaths use mind control to ensnare patients.

How do you already know if you're being managed? The technique being undertaken by means of manner of the use of manipulators can be mentioned in the subsequent chapter. However, here is a little food for idea. Go to a public area (any place in which humans collect) and look around you. How many people do you notice carrying denims? How many people do you notice with the identical hairstyles? Society itself is capable of the use of thoughts manipulate and regularly does with out humans knowing it. Marketing strategies, advertising and marketing and messages in mass media manipulate our alternatives each day. We are creatures of conformity, it appears, and ripe for the selecting thru people who want us to shop for their jeans and use their hair merchandise – even colour our hair a sure color.

Why else can also need to the hairstyles of the 80s have obtained popularity? Certainly no longer non-public flavor. Why else may any female placed on a bubble skirt? Why must any self-respecting guy wear mom jeans – or a mullet? Persistent messages brought via mass communique, mixed with the social vital to suit in, make us at risk of the form of manipulation Wilson Bryan Key become speakme about in his ebook about mass advertising and advertising and consumer way of existence, Subliminal Seduction.

And so with out knowing any humans in my opinion, the mechanisms of alternate pluck us from the gang based mostly on demographic markers like age, gender, income, and the pastimes gleaned from mining our Facebook debts (thanks Zuckerberg!) to aim us as consumers in their products and services.

Consumerism is a cult, too. It's a cult we're all acolytes of in a disposable society wherein planned obsolescence is constructed into every reachable, easy buy. We agree with within the church of the stuff we don't need, because of the truth the television and the net pressure our society within the route of the mall with the unrelenting precision of a pricey GPS gadget. We collaborate willingly, speaking approximately gadgets and vehicles and footwear and the modern-day-day fad in meals you're presupposed to eat (or not purported to devour). We talk approximately it all as even though it were Holy Writ. We are the adherents, basically, of a huge, but unofficial cult.

The club card is to your pockets. It says Visa, or MasterCard, or American Express.

Techniques like viral advertising and advertising and marketing, wherein merchandise are sold to us on the same time as we're engaged in what we think is a web interplay, or a communique in a bar. The subject matter is lightly suggested inside the direction of the products or services on offer and earlier than we recognize it, we've been enlisted in a business hobby's branding and purchaser popularity attempt. We recognize the name of a product we didn't comprehend we wanted and , the call of that product is anywhere we appearance. Just perhaps, the subsequent time we see that call is the time we're able to buy it (irrespective of the truth that we don't really want it).

Viral advertising and advertising has already made it a part of our attention. Without even being conscious that it's taking place, we've were given come to be clients of a product we had no concept existed, till that magic, viral marketing 2nd, which didn't even sense like a profits pitch.

And that's how thoughts control works. You don't see it coming. You're unaware it's happening and , you're setting up your pockets and buying the element you've been endorsed you need to have.

But of all of the institutions that works most actively to manipulate people's minds, some corners of faith are possibly the most egregious examples. Behavior is modified to comply to the "tips" of any given religion, all of the way all of the manner right down to the substances and beverages practitioners can also moreover consume.

The Latin word "cultus" is the muse phrase of the English "cult", this is commonly used to offer an reason for a fringe breakaway enterprise, or a newly-installation non secular faction. Its specific which means, however, is surprising in our current context and the phrase's utilization: the notion in a strength that controls the universe, or veneration of that strength. What this indicates is that the time period is applicable to any and all religious denominations or Faith institutions. Our contemporary usage of the word fails to reflect this, so it's instructive to anticipate in phrases of the phrase's proper usage even as exploring the arena of spiritual "cults". All faith, in essence, suits the real that means of the word.

Religion inside the Form of a Cult

Of the arena's total population, absolutely eighty four% is associated with a spiritual religion. This is a exquisite number and represents eight out of 10 humans. It may be very amusing to have a perception tool. Believing that the arena has a logical center that rewards proper and punishes evil lets in humans to sense stable and regular. Adherents of many Faiths consider they needn't worry demise because an afterlife is promised. They do no longer experience alone due to the fact they believe a better electricity is constantly with them, looking out for them.

What they do not recognise is that faith, in all its bureaucracy, practices a shape of mind control. Think approximately it in this way - whilst you examine the Bible, Qu'ran, or some special ebook considered to be Holy Scripture on your non-public, you interpret it in a sure way. You observe via the passages and assemble your belief machine in keeping with your non-public interpretation of what you've have a look at.

But whilst you attend a residence of worship, the Holy Scripture in play is being interpreted for you via the worship leader. You are suggested what the passages advise via a clergyman, imam, rabbi, and so forth. Whether they've a degree in divinity for his or her unique nook of the spiritual global or now not, Holy Scripture is being filtered through the lens in their ideals, earlier than it gets to you. You are, basically, being requested to surely get hold of the worship leader's interpretation of scripture, in choice to interpreting it yourself. You also can moreover contain your self in a test agency to higher apprehend the scripture of your Faith. But even there, the leader of the corporation will attraction to his or her very very own authority and ultimately, you could start to be for the reason that authority as definitive regarding the translation of scripture.

Perhaps while attending your take a look at business enterprise, you enhance crucial points approximately the scripture you're reading. You find out that the ones are disregarded with the beneficial resource of the have a test chief as invalid. Authority includes a choice what the exceptional interpretation is. Sometimes, that is clearly suitable. However, it's regularly the case that authority in spiritual establishments is misused as a manner to cow practitioners. This is an unfortunate truth of life in institutions — humans with ill cause use the hierarchical structures concerned inside the ones institutions as a way to wield beside the factor power over the organization at massive. Being aware about this tendency and its incidence in hierarchical institutions allow you to keep away from indoctrination proper proper right into a way of wondering that is basically distant places to you. You can avoid it and also you have to.

How to Avoid Indoctrination

For many people, non secular worship is a amazing release from their normal lives. It has a leavening and soothing effect. The liturgy of homes of worship and the communal nature of services can instill in practitioners a feel of belonging to a few element more than themselves. Religious worship additionally gives a rich supply of fellowship, non-public renewal and reflected picture that decorate the lives of tens of millions. However, you must be aware about what it is you in fact believe and keep your right to really be given as proper with it, in a few aspect spiritual context you are in. Being proper to yourself is a vital guiding principle of all religious belief, for in information the self, you may better realise God. If one believes in

God, then honestly the proposition that knowing your self is tantamount to data God, as God (for your belief device) created you. That approach your middle ideals aren't inside the market to any worship leader who attempts to make you accept as true with that they're incorrect, or one way or the other unsound in conflict of words of his very own.

At times, human beings turn out to be fairly worried of their spiritual institutions. This can each decorate or intrude with their lives. Greater involvement may be very profitable, regarding work with the terrible and ill. It can take you out of yourself and result in you to pursue sports activities which may be fantastic and beneficial to your network. However, this identical involvement can end up a problem in the presence of a manipulative community leader, bent on organization conformity to the problem that he desires preferred ideological settlement alongside collectively along with his personal schedule.

All humans are born with the right to freedom of spiritual notion. This is expressed within the UN Charter of Human Rights. That way you've got the proper to interpret the scriptures of your Faith tradition in line with your non-public, middle values. This is an hassle among you and God and no person else. It's not your worship leader's company to interfere with that relationship. A worship leader is in place to guide, no longer name for and no longer manage the minds of his flock. If you revel in that your worship chief is jogging to intrude with the middle ideals of your network, you need to now not most effective withstand, you need to actively paintings in that network to counter the effect. Should the trouble be persistent and entrenched, it's honestly useful to vicinity an give up to that leadership's have an impact on by means of taking your concerns to a person at a higher stage of the group. This won't commonly paintings, but it's generally without a doubt really worth the strive, if you enjoy that a frontrunner is abusing his electricity.

The abuse of energy can show up in any institution, but non secular ones seem particularly liable to it. Power may be wielded to protect spiritual leaders from scrutiny with the useful resource of way of the community he's charged with or maybe, the law of the land. A appropriate example of that is the pedophile scandal inside the Roman Catholic Church.

Leaders of that agency actively sought to shield clergymen responsible of abuse via manner of transferring them from diocese to diocese and parish to parish. Simply, revelation of those crimes would possibly have had the power to break the agency and so practitioners have been lied to and managed via the use of distortions of the church's teachings. Further the traditional energy structures of the Church's hierarchy were abused on the best degree. Priests, bishops, archbishops and cardinals all labored to hold this scandal from the area's hobby till Catholics should now not fake it wasn't taking area.

This scandal maximum probably introduced approximately the resignation of Benedict XVI (a completely uncommon Papal resignation; some element not seen for hundreds of years) and has compelled the living Pope to begin the device of investigating the slew of court times that has accumulated over time.

The abuse of energy within the RCC pedophile scandal is an notable example of what can occur whilst spiritual leaders abuse their authority. Beginning with their patients, clergymen abused their authority to prey on kids of their congregations. This abuse became compounded through the usage of an business enterprise-significant conspiracy to hide the ones crimes from public view via shuttling the accountable parties to unique locations. In factor, the ones moves have been spurred thru the church's very own theology of the priesthood – that one is born a clergyman and one dies a priest, even though the priest is prolonged to the papacy. This makes defrocking extremely hard.

A further wrinkle on this story of mass mind manipulate and the abuse of power that stems from it, is conduct on the very pleasant stages of the church. This involved submitting to blackmail, constant with Fr. Robert Hoatson, who modified into responsible for unmasking as a minimum a part of the scandal. Fr. Hoatson claimed that pedophile priests blackmailed gay Archbishops with a view to keep their status. Again, the church's very own theology changed into its worst enemy, because the RCC has (till very currently) taken a completely rigid stance on sexuality.

You can see how topics may spiral out of all manipulate – but no longer the control of Catholic minds, which compelled the silence of sufferers and their families all over the worldwide for lots extended years.

But memories like the ones play out internationally, in all its religions. At the idea of it's miles the abuse of strength and the use of strict control of humans's mind and movements, because of their reputation of that power's primacy and their worry of hard it.

Religious cults, with the stern needs made from their fans, are ripe for this type of abuse. As stated above, men like Jim Jones and David Koresh knew this to be actual and actually used that facts to their benefit as a way to advantage standard manage over their fanatics. As for his know-how of the Bible, Koresh definitely had little or no and had truely no instructional analyzing underneath his belt. He located what he knew at his church, using his remarkable capacity for rote memorization. He did, but, have a totally specific interpretive present, which endeared him to fans.

In the founding of the Branch Davidian cult, David Koresh claimed to have had a direct revelation from God, concerning the Seven Seals of the Book of Revelation, and that God had "anointed" him to teach approximately what they meant.

His fans have been informed what to consume, whilst to devour and had been punished for no longer doing as he informed. He may from time to time trade the recommendations, claiming he'd been directed to with the beneficial useful resource of God. Both feared and cherished, his fanatics believed all he stated and because of that notion had been powerless to behave contrary to his commands.

This introduced about his abuse of young women for his non-public, sexual gratification. He took them as "better halves", compelling them to put on a pendant with a "w" engraved on it to signify that they have been married to him and have been completely devoted to him and no special guy in the cult. The parents of those women, as adherents of the cult must do now not something however stand through and watch as their daughters were abused. This is the power of thoughts manage, at the same time as maliciously finished with the useful resource of people like Koresh – fans lose their power, their morals and their functionality to think independently.

When mixed with religious belief, mind manipulate is a powerful tool for humans with an eye fixed to abusing strength thru controlling the thoughts and movements of others.

Chapter 2: The Mind Control Process

In most instances, the number one intention of manipulators is to create a similar to themselves - to have the contributors of the cult think like them. To reap this, one want to have a immoderate experience of entitlement and a properly-fed ego. Having no doubt in oneself is the critical component to having the ability to steer people that one is above authority and ought to be emulated. In notable phrases, cult leaders will enforce a extremely-present day character on their sufferers.

Everyone can fall prey to this form of manipulation, and it's miles best a rely of the way big the mind manage is that's being imposed that determines its very last fulfillment, or how profoundly it will alternate its patients.

Almost all manipulators look at a chain of steps to efficaciously impose their will on one-of-a-type human beings. This has been confirmed over and over via way of the many networking and advertising agencies which actively recruit people to sell their merchandise. All new humans undergo a scientific education about the way to recruit regardless of the truth that more human beings and the way to compel goal customers to make a buy. This way correlates to that of thoughts manipulate in its success and power.

A primary outline of the thoughts manage technique is provided and described beneath.

Reading People
Of direction, in advance than something else, the agent have to establish a connection or bond with their sufferer. As defined earlier than, with friendship as the foundation of a dating, all mental and social defenses of sufferers can be lowered. Intimacy offers get admission to to the agent, due to the fact the purpose harbors no suspicions. Having received the reason's take into account, the manipulative agent gets to art work finding strategies and method of wielding manage.

Manipulators typically will test capacity dreams that allows you to reach at a selection to truly aim them. They need to recognise that the character they're inspecting (like a malicious program underneath a magnifying glass) is liable to their manipulations. They need to recognize that this is the case earlier than making efforts to bond with them, as doing so might be a waste of time, if have been there no ability for manipulation.

Body language, verbal clues, the lean of a head, the use of the hands – those types of are essential records which tell others what form of man or woman you're. Do you have got self-self notion? Are you shy? Are you sturdy? Are you prone? Extrovert? Introvert? We all provide plenty about ourselves away while interacting with distinctive human beings and the expert manipulator is nicely aware about this. The arch manipulator will search for signs and symptoms and signs and symptoms and signs which you're going to be a cooperative intention; symptoms and signs and symptoms and signs and symptoms like arms folded for the duration of your frame as despite the fact that hugging your self, that may advise you're insecure. They observe posture – is it formidable and confident, or inclined and bowed? Large strides when walking can in truth sign a notable loss of self assurance. Blinking can mean you're lying.

There is lots data you're generating by using the usage of in reality being within the international, that it may pay to be aware of the indicators your frame is sending. (More on reading the body language of others and curating you personal, later in this e-book).

In scoping out capacity goals, the agent entails understand the person's viable weaknesses, interests, and strengths, and makes use of those to end up aware about regions of vulnerability. Knowing a capacity intention has get proper of access to elements that may be exploited for the agent's manipulative cause is vital to determine whether or no longer to continue with bonding in the direction of controlling and manipulating the eventual purpose.

How do they try this? Generally, marketers will test out a person thru first impressions, and this assessment is amply served via frame language. People all have 3 personas:

(1) Private Persona,
(2) Public Persona, and
(3) Reputation.

The first is the mirrored image of the real, internal persona. It is the person who lives internal his head, and is composed of thoughts, attitudes, possibilities, hopes, desires, values and emotions. The second is the person people venture to the arena. Here, effective dispositions are conspicuously displayed, at the same time as negative ones are mitigated. The zero.33 one is how others perceive the man or woman character; that may be a few component none parents has a whole lot manage over. These 3 personas are the muse of the primary affect. As they're announcing (and it in truth jewelry actual) – first impressions are lasting impressions.

Agents may be capable of pretty rapidly take a look at the information you unwittingly provide and check out your fee and usability as a aim. If they discover you appropriate to their manipulative makes use of, or inside the event that they suppose you can display to be an obedient follower, they may then hold reading your strengths, weaknesses, insecurities, goals, values, and some thing they may be able to use as leverage. Afterwards, based on their assessment of you, they may redesign themselves into the self-example they agree with will maximum attraction to you to make certain your hobby and to advantage your believe. All of the agent's actions will deliver the ones 4 easy messages:

➤ I like your man or woman.
➤ We are the identical.
➤ You can take delivery of as authentic with me.
➤ We are proper for each exquisite.

Of route, there are times at the same time as all the steps stated above might not look at every unique in strict series. Some may additionally moreover overlap, at the same time as others may moreover moreover change places in the way. Changes to the same old strolling way of the manipulator depend upon the situation and a excellent manipulator will revel in making the crucial calibrations. Nonetheless, those comprise step one of the mind manage approach -- putting in a connection and instilling take transport of as actual with inside the goal.

Unfreezing
Everyone has a semi-constant set of values and ideals amassed due to the fact that youth. We carry those with us into maturity, sometimes including to them, or revising them as we flow

along. But lots of those values and beliefs are immutable. They have become a part of our identities. When those values and beliefs are referred to as into question, contradicted, or threatened, our herbal reaction is to defend the ones carefully held beliefs as part of who we're. Because they'll be.

When we're compelled to question the ones installation values and beliefs ourselves, because of the manipulation of some other man or woman, or via manner of manner of life times, we're present process what is called "unfreezing". Many situations can reason this; the lack of a loved one, being fired from a undertaking, or repossession of a house. Anything that reasons us to are seeking out solutions and to in all likelihood query our center beliefs about how lifestyles works, or why we're right right right here; to impeach traditional mind approximately society and the manner it capabilities – all these suggest that we're encountering a shift in a totally essential part of ourselves. We are, in essence, unfreezing crucial middle values and ideals which have been thrown into doubt via the usage of circumstance – or the machinations of a manipulator.

Going through a length of emotional vulnerability which compels changes to our rate tool makes us extra available as targets to manipulative human beings and similarly indicates that we're willing. We turn out to be perfect fodder for manipulators. As defined in advance, manipulators use the weaknesses of different people to their gain, and they'll say anything their dreams need or need to pay attention.

A commonplace example of this is at the same time as a robust-minded guy enters a romantic dating with a lady who has very little self-confidence. He insists in implementing his will on her at the pretext that he loves her, cherishes her and desires to defend her. Often, in relationships which consist of this, the stronger accomplice (whether or now not it's the person) will recognise all of the proper matters to mention that allows you to obtain power over the weaker partner and to feel on pinnacle of things.

But it's not honestly in romantic relationships that manipulation takes vicinity. All relationships are situation to power dynamics. Vulnerability and a lack of self-self assure or arrogance are invites to the manipulators of this global, even in our very very personal families, in which parents manipulate children and vice versa.

The Process

The fundamental purpose of this diploma is to unweave the aim from his past, due to the fact this may allow the agent to compel the aim to allow pass of his mounted values and beliefs, and cleave to those of his manipulator. Apart from this distancing, however, the agent can even make the preceding sports activities in the sufferer's lifestyles appear horrible, incorrect, or the purpose of all their hardships. This manner, the target will have no way of protecting himself or his know-how of the sector in advance than the manipulator commenced to do his artwork. This renders the intention susceptible to accepting new requirements and ideas by using deliberate deposit on the a part of the agent.

As for the techniques utilized in mind manipulate, it's essential that the victim be remoted from the out of doors worldwide to the best degree viable, at some stage inside the technique. This method the agent will make complete use of seminars, recognition organisation discussions, or perhaps one-on-

one meet-united states of america of americain the manipulator's territory.

In the case of a manipulator who has set up a friendship for features apart from indoctrination proper into a advertising and advertising and marketing and advertising scheme or cult, the agent will make sure as plenty touch as viable alongside together with his purpose and as little with notable pals and family as feasible. This will growth his opportunity to deposit his values in the reason closer to his stop (whether than quit be financial gain, or genuinely the amusing of controlling a few exceptional character). If feasible, it's miles proper to area the target within the agent's environment twenty-4 hours an afternoon to have strict manipulate over the goal's sports activities sports. There are some who will intentionally weaken the victim's frame thru proscribing and restricting their meals intake. This is a common practice in cults, however also can be visible in abusive romantic and family relationships. Often, the pretext of taking place a weight loss plan collectively can be used. Meanwhile, the agent might be consuming what he constantly eats, without the purpose's data.

Some strategies require the victim to take part within the thoughts manipulate machine past due at night time time. The thoughts is worn-out during those hours, causing the goal to bypass critical wondering and to absolutely take shipping of as real with some factor is being stated through the manipulator. In cults, this could be coupled with public confessions -- likely the most effective tactic to unfreeze sufferers. The purpose loses his experience of privacy, merging with the company in an awful manner. This makes him greater prone to special techniques of thoughts manage.

Keep in mind that each one personal statistics can and may be used to break the intention's will. Humiliation and insult could be expressed subtly via the agent (whether or not leading a hard and fast, or acting one-on-one). This method instills in the goal a sense of self-doubt. Targets start to question their hold close of reality and because of this and is thrown into an unbalanced country of private turmoil. In the case of a cult, installed members serve the undertaking of de-stabilizing the aim's experience of self with the aid of reinforcing the message being delivered. In the case of human beings enduring this way, it's miles subtler, with the agent taking notably extra time, in a much

much less vast manner, to de-stabilize and instill doubt in his motive.

During this degree, the dealers will introduce the solution to the intention's misgivings. They will gift their ideology as the solution to the motive's problems. If the manipulator is focused on a group, and any people of the company have enough feel in them left to oppose or query the ideology being instilled, those contributors might be isolated or further defamed. They can be made an instance which exceptional people; weaker humans, may be loath to conform with.

Of direction, some desires select out to transport away the companies which exercising manipulation in their very non-public accord, and dealers may not prevent them from doing so. In reality, this can even assist assist the cause of the manipulator in query. The agent will use this act as a manner to uplift the spirits of the very last organization individuals with the aid of the usage of pronouncing that the individual that walked out isn't however organized to surely be given the higher non secular calling they offer. He will say that individuals who stay have advanced beyond the extent of the departing goal, or have chosen the more intelligent route.

In the grip of effective feelings, the purpose is probably hard pressed to think significantly. This is precisely the country manipulators want to collect in their goals. Once goals are experiencing distress, the way is apparent to influence dreams inside the route of ecstatic reports, and/or the belief that the agent is the solution to all their issues. By this factor, desires will need no longer something greater than for their hell of self-doubt and instability to save you and could do whatever to move beyond it – which consist of succumbing to the ideological urgings of the agent.

Peer strain is some other approach used by dealers of mind control and manipulation. Exposure to the manipulator's surroundings inside the context of a hard and fast will follow the ones 3 easy, unspoken policies:

➢ The intention will do regardless of the agent wishes, inside the the front of others.
➢ After doing it, the incident can be constant inside the goal's thoughts.
➢ Since the incident is fixed in the purpose's thoughts, he is going to accept as true with he

did what he was commanded to do thru the agent of his private volition.

And as described in advance, while targets come to the problem of the thoughts control technique at which they be given as authentic with their actions are being completed as a byproduct in their personal will and not that of the agent, they may be reaching thoughts manage's apogee (low element – or immoderate factor, in case you're the agent). At this degree of the game, the resistance of goals is diminished to nearly no longer some thing and they're now creatures of the agent's designs.

Freezing

The pseudo-character will start to shape on this stage of the thoughts manage manner. However, hold in mind that the strategies used beneath unfreezing, the technique, and freezing will normally overlap. The order of those levels is largely depending on how sufferers respond to the mind manipulate technique, as a whole. Nonetheless, all through the freezing diploma, the intention undergoes a catastrophic inner conflict, as his vintage and new identities war.

In order to solidify the values and beliefs being instilled via the manipulator, the equal reward/punishment method used on kids and animals is hired. Good behaviors are rewarded via smooth however quite-prized privileges (a one-on-one speak with the chief, involvement in a making plans method, or a special identify, permission to call domestic, or maybe a visit).

Punishments, however, are fast, however harsh. Depending on how awful the victim's conduct is, punishments will range from dropping management duties, public insults, or guidelines on speaking or eating. Physical beatings can also be a part of the punishment, but, of direction, now not all cult businesses bypass this a ways with punishment. The identical form of praise/punishment schema can be seen in non-public relationships. As said, those are often hired in childrearing, however can be visible in romantic relationships, friendships and in offices, as a good deal as and collectively with the employment of violence to punish unwelcome behavior.

Keep in thoughts that regardless of being physical mistreated through his manipulator, the purpose willingly accepts punishment as what he merits. The mind manipulate hired

44

thru the agent has instilled in the intention a belief that justice is being served, even if it makes no experience to a person searching on from outdoor the context of the relationship. Women who're beaten through the use of manipulative guys, as an example, offer an reason for staying with the ones abusive men because they believed that they might be killed, lose their children, or that that they'd little charge out of doors the confines of the abusive courting. This is also mind manipulate and employed within the identical style as it's far in business employer situations. Carrot and stick are fashionable as devices of the agent's justice (despite the fact that the stick is hired violently).

Another method of freezing the pseudo-individual of desires is to have them version it. As discussed in advance, the goal of mind manage is to create a duplicate of the agent, or to embody the agent's beliefs of the way the area is, in his thoughts, through the cause. There is not any quicker manner to do this than to have humans go out and recruit greater human beings. By doing this, humans of the business enterprise speak with the agent's voice, modelling his ideology with a purpose to disseminate his message. Selling the concept will, in truth, require the people to be in reality invested in it.

Re-indoctrination additionally can be beneficial in freezing the pseudo-individual. This is why a few companies require individuals to wait seminars or camps each week, month, or 12 months, counting on the 'qualifications' of the organization.

The mind manage device is slow, (specially in a unmarried-on-one conditions) and may take years for it to honestly take root. Once it does, but, it'll take a commensurate amount of time to undo, and can require expert help to virtually dislodge from the psyche of the cause.

The effects of thoughts manage aren't past healing help. As prolonged because the goal is removed completely from the surroundings wherein thoughts manipulate has been perpetrated, and follows a diligent path to recuperation, with the help of a capable and compassionate therapist, complete recuperation is almost continuously feasible.

Many query why it's far that a few humans live in manipulative dating. But human beings in a state of affairs in which they're being subjected to mind control depend on the person who is controlling their mind. Targets don't see leaving as an possibility (as noted above, in the instance of abused and battered ladies), in spite of the reality that the abusive conduct they're enduring is unacceptable to others. You may also sincerely have been in a scenario like this and feature presented this e-book to attempt to keep away from getting into that situation over again. If that's the case, examine on. The statistics contained within the following chapters you could locate particularly useful. This statistics may also be useful for all and sundry hoping to benefit more manage in their lives and the actions of the people in it.

Chapter 3: Mind Control Techniques

The thoughts manipulate method described in the preceding bankruptcy is direct and usually used by organizations or cults of all sizes. There are many conspiracy theories fluttering about at the net, social media, and the likes about mind manage being practiced on a country wide, or perhaps global, scale. When thinking about the techniques stated, it could seem now not viable to complete that the government, corporations and the elite are, in truth, manipulating the masses. That is due to the surreptitious strategies via using which they're able to attain the same effect as extra overt sorts of thoughts manipulate.

These gamers are all about power. They're now not interested by selecting people's pockets, masses as they'll be in other ends. It's greater about maintaining anybody in line and in their proper places. By inculcating conformity via some of channels, it will become a extremely good deal less tough to achieve the compliance of the masses. In distinct phrases, as a way to accumulate the stableness of the device, it's critical to instill within the population the price of conforming to wonderful beliefs about the way the region is. Though it could not sound as terrible due to the fact we due to the fact we typically tend to apprehend the concept of order in a first-class manner, what makes their strategies questionable is the truth that they impair people's capability to think drastically for you to acquire this surrender. In common with the way described inside the previous bankruptcy, everyone is underneath the effect that they've made their very own alternatives; that they're dwelling their lives as impartial folks who make their non-public options. But the reality is that mass media has undermined many people's ability to do this. With the degradation of language associated with the facts age (a drastic reduce fee within the variety of those who examine books, texting, passive viewing), we also are rapidly losing our capability to call what's incorrect.

Most of the strategies used to control humans are very familiar. If you're an average citizen, then you may be rather aware of them, and you may have felt the impact of this have an impact on to your very very own lifestyles.

Education

A systematic and organized form of training is the proper mind controlling method. Any must-be dictator or tyrant might easily call on it inside the provider of huge scale indoctrination.

Witness how Hitler managed to instill his ideals and beliefs on German minors within the direction of his reign thru the Hitler Youth, the use of applications of mass schooling and indoctrination. Existing educational infrastructure can come to be a cornerstone of authoritarian ideologies, stressful complete conformity to a fixed of beliefs that serves the united states, from the ones enrolled. This method of thoughts control is pretty effective, manipulating the choice for reputation through achievement, praise/punishment and peer tracking.

At any early degree in lifestyles, the charge of coaching youngsters to obey and not to deviate from the deposit of the data supplied through the gadget is especially beneficial to the behavior of authoritarianism. Instilling the want to conform from an early age creates a basis for the continuing health of such regimes and ensures their ongoing grip on electricity. Deposit schooling, crafted to provide a thoughts-set which serves the kingdom's preference for willing squaddies, an administrative elegance and other operatives, precludes the need for thinking outdoor the confines of that device of concept. The pupil will become a creature of his schooling and the schooling a part of the creature. If the educational gadget teaches its students that, as an example, "greed is right", the ones youngsters will develop up believing that they need to pursue coins and wealth earlier than all exclusive worries, because of the fact it's far the right factor to do. Questioning the assertions made will now not even get up to the successfully indoctrinated pupil.

The purpose of training isn't to grind out carbon reproduction people who are not able to assume for themselves. In reality, the purpose of training is to create an knowledgeable elegance capable of innovating and growing societal particular for the advantage of all. In an authoritarian governmental shape, the inhibition of critical thinking, then, does not serve the united states of america, in any respect. Rather, it undermines the united states of the united states within the provider of a very small elite, which exploits the uneducated mass. Unable to anticipate itself out of the state of affairs, the mass knowledgeable thru deposit of authoritarian ideology can not spoil free with out catastrophic events, just like the autumn of the Third Reich. This left Germany devastated and the world over despised. It took whole disintegrate for the thrall of instructional indoctrination and relentless government propaganda to be damaged and for reality to take maintain.

Propaganda and Advertising
Large-scale thoughts manipulate, at the same time as sugarcoated, is called advertising and advertising and marketing. This field in exchange is solely targeted on knowledge what the masses want and want, (or perhaps telling them what they want and want) and a manner to get into people's heads an excellent manner to promote them subjects. The precept weapon of advertising and marketing is advertising and marketing and propaganda. Despite employing quick, easy to absorb messages, the way advertising and marketing and advertising depends and composed is focused on conveying messages powerful sufficient to transport human beings and make them do what's desired — especially, to buy products and services.

Subliminal Seduction
Wilson Bryan Key's groundbreaking 1974 ebook as regards to advertising and advertising and advertising and marketing and mass marketing blew the lid off the practices of the corporation. In its pages, Key found out the subliminal messages regularly included inside the

advertising and marketing of the day. Sexual imagery and its power to influence had been the focal point of this, with Key claiming its covert use in marketing and advertising pictures to influence public searching for picks.

But wrapped inside the sexual message (existence), were additionally messages and images which elicited a pretty a completely unique reaction in the consumer. Also being protected in advertising and marketing and advertising and marketing had been snap shots that subliminally recalled the inevitability of demise. An implicit risk, nearly, even as juxtaposed with sexual imagery, loss of existence imagery served as a strong goad to customer conduct.

While Key's work has been criticized in contemporary many years, his assertions of hidden messages in marketing and advertising and marketing had been not the primary. In 1957, Vance Packard's The Hidden Persuaders further warned of the mental studies advertising and marketing businesses frequently undertook in order to arrive at effective advertising and marketing and advertising schemes. It observed that marketing and advertising and marketing executives used psychology with the intention to more convincingly appeal to customers on behalf in their organisation clients. This quantity emerge as published proper away earlier than an test done thru researcher James Vickery inside the identical 12 months. In the test, Vickery examined the efficacy of flashing suggestive words onto the screen of a movie theater in New Jersey. Suggestions like "drink Coca-Cola" and "consume popcorn" were flashed at the display screen all through the jogging of movies in advance than 14,000 site traffic, over the route of the take a look at.

Only validated for 1/3000th of a second every, Vickery located that the messages progressed profits for Coke via 57% inside the course of the direction of the test. Popcorn profits increased with the aid of 18%.

But Vickery, lamentably, later admitted that he'd doctored his research data and cutting-edge-day pupils are rather reluctant to provide a splendid deal of credence to the thoughts of Key, in his writings. All the same, it's clean that marketing is well known to be manipulative.

As early as 1896, despite the fact that, the concept of influencing mass conduct and the way it is probably executed has grow to be part of highbrow and scientific exploration. Gustave le Bon's The Crowd became an early exploration of this effect, reading how it come to be that large numbers of people can be inspired to engage in "agency expect" and be held inside the thrall of intellectually proscribing thoughts and ideologies.

Viral advertising and advertising and marketing, as an example, is based upon on patron purchase in in numerous arenas so that you can unfold the message. Budweiser, as an instance, has been very a success in encouraging Facebook clients to percentage its heartwarming classified ads providing Clydesdale horses and puppies (who doesn't like dogs?). The movies are so powerful that no character sharing them appears to object to taking element within the advertising of a corporation this is having its interest executed free of price.

Branding on apparel moreover has a powerful effect on customer behavior. There is little reluctance at the part of clients to place on apparel emblazoned with brand names. In impact, they have made taking walks billboards of themselves and feature in reality paid for the privilege to reap this. What is probably more effective? Your emblem call isn't great displayed freed from rate; you are making a earnings on the same time as customers are doing the approach for you.

In an age of mass communication and a 24/7 records glut, it's frequently hard to determine even as it's miles we're being marketed to. Advertising messages are definitely disguised as first-rate content, unthinkingly shared by using using heaps and thousands throughout more than one systems. If splendid for this contemporary twist on subliminal messaging, it's controversial that Keys, while a controversial determine within the international of communications scholarship, changed into proper.

Religion, Politics, and Sports

These companies all, to a tremendous quantity, interact in thoughts manage. By dividing humans into camps of loyalty, human beings are pitted closer to every other. In the sector of sports sports, loyalties are fierce, but the worldwide of hobby is more approximately enjoyment. When your organization is a political party, or a spiritual Faith, the kind of loyalty modelled with the aid of sports fans for their respective organizations can grow to be dangerous and virulent. "Go crew" will become allow's bomb Iraq, for one. It becomes "the pink hazard". It becomes the Final Solution.

Oppositionalism in the ones arenas affords a colourful floor for retaining humans divided. When people are divided, there may be little hazard they may be able to unite spherical an concept – like crushing the global banking device, or preventing weather change, for example. As all of us skip about keeping petty grudges over our institution losing a game, an election, a war, or a race to build up more adherents to our Faith, the humans on the top of the pyramid have amusing. As lengthy as we're stored busy with our internecine squabbles, their manipulate is confident.

Recently, memes (photo messages) have surfaced on Facebook, showing huge companies of human beings engaged in celebrations of sports activities activities victories. These memes ask an vital query – what might occur if all the human beings on this photograph carried out themselves to uniting over some thing possibly greater essential that sports activities? What if these types of masses of human beings of their group jerseys, in location of whooping it up within the streets of important cities over a game, crammed the streets in protest over the systematic accumulation of wealth at the top of the meals chain?

This may want to not serve folks that is probably served – no longer you and I, in extraordinary phrases. Our distractions serve them. They create a form of myopia in which the large photograph (the high-quality in which our lives have emerge as increasingly much plenty less a hit and prosperous; even extra hopeless) is obscured from our view. We can't unite to venture them, because we are able to't see them thru our group-coloured glasses.

As for the phantasm of choice, the top notch instance might be the grocery keep. In the grocery store (which has emerge as larger and greater diverse in its business more in modern some years than everybody may moreover want to ever have imagined), we're assaulted with the aid of way of infinite choice. Which shampoo will make our hair shinier? Which breakfast cereal gets our time without work to a better start? Which relaxation room bowl cleanser will leave the porcelain most spotlessly smooth and clean smelling? Each of these gadgets has myriad incarnations, all from competing manufacturers. Some of these brands are even owned via the identical companies, pushing a whole lot of products. Disguised as desire, a marketplace complete of labels that claim advanced capacity over all others call for that we buy them. They name to us, saying they'll make our lives better. Whole aisles of grocery shops are devoted to severa kinds of potato chips, in every flavor from salt and vinegar to rib eye steak. But it's all an phantasm, due to the reality regardless of what we purchase, even on the very excellent cease of the dizzying array on provide, the give up end end result will not be extra dramatically unique than if we'd provided the neighboring bottle at the shelf (for a whole lot plenty much less coins). It's all the equal. It's all what it's miles. It all does the equal hobby. Only the labels are top notch, in an attempt to entice the coins out of our pockets within the quest for shinier hair and greater energizing smelling toilet bowls.

There is nothing, basically, wrong with the concept of preference. What's incorrect is the masquerade. There isn't whatever wrong with mission, faith or politics. It's the masquerade; the illusion that deprives us of right picks and compels us to be anxious over affairs that function distractions from extra vital subjects.

The golden rule is found in each spiritual Faith in the worldwide and but we having been slaughtering every one of a kind for eons over whose god is the bigger, higher god. Every political birthday celebration claims to have the answers we are looking for for to our economic woes, but the structures wherein they function defy improvement. Political donations, lobbying and the company impact these represent make the behavior of our affairs a depend of sale to the very great bidder.

Yet, we're so busy cheering on our crew, we don't word. Perhaps that because the television is ever murmuring in the historic beyond, telling us our hair isn't excellent enough and our toilet bowl doesn't fragrance glowing sufficient.

Food, Water and Air

One of the finest debates currently going on is spherical genetically changed plant life and different meals sources. The present day-day reputation through the Federal Department of Agriculture of GMO salmon suggests they're now not going anywhere.

The production of meals has turn out to be so systematic and commercialized that it now is based on numerous chemical fertilizers and insecticides and unnatural techniques to deliver sufficient food for a developing population. At least, that's what we're informed. But the reality is that there's properly enough food. The trouble lies in a market ascendency annoying large profits for less strive, in less turnaround time. Because of this, meals being provided almost everywhere consists of pollutants and poisons that could adjust the mind's chemistry and human physical fitness.

Outbreaks of illnesses in agency chook (avian flu) and pork (bovine spongiform encephalitis, or "mad cow illness"), in addition to spates of inflamed veggies and dairy products plague our now closely adulterated meals systems. The problem is the rush to market, a lack of regulation in plenty of markets (america, specially) and the greed which has occasioned every those realities in meals manufacturing.

GMOs aren't necessarily a terrible detail. Factory farming isn't, every. It's the way wherein a few companies pursue those activities that's at hassle. GMOs, if administered beneath the watchful eye of a vigilant government, can provide worldwide food safety. In a worldwide of employer have an impact on using de-regulation, however, that is not the case. The identical is real of manufacturing unit farming. In the absence of true enough authorities regulation and vigilance, producers interact in unethical, cruel and unsanitary practices that endanger our food property. Of direction, whilst we're cheering on the agency, we continue to be ignorant of those pressing traumatic situations.

Mass mind control is primarily based upon on our inattention and that has now been performed to this form of diploma, that we now not even recognize what we're feeding our children, or ourselves.

Religion serves an essential function in society and whilst now not abused for political abilities, like marginalizing minorities, or interfering within the behavior of elections (because it maximum really is, with beautiful regularity). In the bosom of a Faith gadget, many find out a enjoy of belonging and motive. It also can't be disregarded that many non secular institutions spend a extraordinary deal of money and time in the direction of feeding, educating, housing and otherwise making lives greater tolerable for masses of masses of human beings round the world. Sikh temples, as an instance, host weekly food at which all are welcome to come back and eat. This is a social company, out of doors authorities, run virtually by the temples which serves to lighten the burden of presidency in feeding hungry humans. Many church buildings, mosques and synagogues carry out similar features.

This doesn't endorse that non secular establishments aren't ripe hiding locations for manipulators. They maximum clearly are (as discussed earlier). In a few spiritual institutions, practitioners are tightly controlled with the useful resource of the use of religious leaders. Followers who do no longer adhere to the suggestions set down via network leaders can be excommunicated. This can suggest being remoted from circle of relatives and pals, similarly to traditional social isolation. Many maintain for years to paste to the strictures in their spiritual framework due to the concern of ostracism.

Manipulation and thoughts manipulate have best the end reason of retaining a dating of domination with the goal. This is real regardless of the context wherein it's practiced. The goal, having been made to enjoy more secure in the controlling situation than out of doors its confines, will stay because of the illusion of protection and belonging provided inner it. Women stay with abusive husbands. Cult participants live in an abusive cult with risky or maybe detrimental ideals. People tolerate otherwise untenable conditions because the opportunity is scary. Having misplaced their functionality to purpose; their vital questioning competencies, they live and live abused and manipulated.

As we're growing, every person acquire messages that could stay with us at some point of our lives. Imagine collectively with non secular or political indoctrination. We trust we appearance awesome in a sure sort of get dressed, due to the fact we've recommended it's what's perfect, or what's "in fashion". We go along with it, due to the reality absolutely everyone else is wearing this form of dress. Looking back at photographs of ourselves, we ask ourselves "What modified into I questioning?". We can't take delivery of as proper with we'd ever go out in public looking like that, but having been glad that no longer to reap this must negatively impact our public picture, we circulate alongside. We internalize the messages, specially even as we're more younger, to our private detriment.

People are however living who participated within the systematic persecution of Black humans within the United States, due to the reality they were traumatic an forestall to the Jim Crow criminal guidelines, which restricted their constitutional rights. Some humans hold in mind the movies and pictures of the technology with horror. Others look returned on it as yet each distinct bankruptcy inside the defeat of the South inside the Civil War. There are humans who've been raised with the perception that they will be superior with the aid of precise function of the color in their skin, their sex, their nationality, their political association, their faith, the coloration in their eyes. These ideals are instilled from the cradle and are the most tough to shake free.

If you consider mind manipulate isn't part of your existence already, mirror on a number of what you've virtually take a look at. You'll see that's in no way the case. Take a check the goods you purchase, the religion you study and the training you've had. Think about famous beliefs which have been exceeded without delay to you on your adolescents and the manner the ones beliefs stack up nowadays. Do you still accept as true with them? Do you observed the arena has spun out of control and you're the final of the sane humans? Or probable you understand now that those beliefs weren't serving you and feature amended them to extra well mirror the truth you stay in.

Somewhere in your existence, you can see evidence of thoughts manage, whether or not or not you want to admit to it or not. We are managed with the aid of the environment wherein we stay and the influences which might be delivered to go through within that environment. What we see and pay attention round us are formative impacts, particularly if we're youngsters.

Being aware about the ones affects is useful and instructive and can help you think extensively approximately your personal beliefs and vicinity inside the world. That focus additionally will let you in gaining knowledge of to put in exercise the manipulate of those round you that permits you to help you in lifestyles. This may be a first rate manner and a force for alternate. We'll find out this within the subsequent monetary break.

Chapter 4: Controlling People With Your Mind

Mind manage needn't constantly be employed to unwell effect, or to harm others. There are tactics in which thoughts manage can be applied to the area round you constructively and helpfully. You and people round you may truely benefit from understanding a way to use it responsibly. As said in advance, mind manage may be used to assist remedy addiction or even despair. Furthermore, expertise the basics of manipulation can assist every body gain extraordinary adjustments and results, like:

➢ Calming down a brewing combat.
➢ Helping a pal affected by despair.
➢ Escaping the worst excesses of the place of work manager.
➢ Saving a falling marriage.
➢ Raising responsible and socially conscious youngsters.
➢ Influencing others to do pinnacle in the international.
➢ Convincing others to sign up for a worth motive.

There are many situations in which thoughts manipulate may be carried out. Using the power of your mind to exchange conditions for the higher is right aspect of manipulation (which has a awful name). Learning the way to finesse conditions to reap a effective outcome is a properly really worth pursuit. They say you want to alternate the world one individual at a time.

Here's your risk!
Know the Personality of the Person You're Dealing With
The first steps of the use of mind manipulate techniques with human beings are just like the ones used by cults to lure recruits into their ranks — with the aid of the usage of looking on the person in query and discerning individual traits. Seeing how people deal with their feelings (specially in conflict conditions), is a manner to glean clues approximately this.
There are a number of various factors which have to be taken into consideration, as well. Think approximately your desires. Why could possibly you want or need to govern the thoughts of this man or woman? What are your intentions? And what are the effects you're hoping for?

You need to noticeably ask yourself these questions, as one-of-a-type individual types will reply in any other case in your techniques. Is your supposed target lured by monetary benefit, or the capability for some shape of reward? When you recognize the character of your goal, you start to see the path through the use of which your thoughts control is probably simplest.

Examining the reason's frame language, verbal clues, hand gestures and the sort of language he uses to your interactions with him. All those will provide you with a top notch deal of information approximately the personality in play.

Four Basic Personality Colors
Network marketers frequently categorize people into four types; those driven thru pity (yellow), through information (inexperienced), via the usage of the usage of familiarity (blue), and in the long run, the ones pushed with the useful resource of opposition (red). Marketers, in coming near capacity clients, first initiate small communicate to assess beneath which of these four classes the capacity consumer belongs. When they have got an idea approximately this, they will tailor their pitch to

their perception about the person's center motivations.

To convince yellow human beings to buy, marketers want to use language like "for charity", "to help a chum", and similar motivations. Yellows are people immoderate in empathy. To have the ability to steer them to purchase a product, no matter the fact that it is clean they do now not want it, they need to be assured their buy benefits a motive or extra motive.

People within the inexperienced elegance base their shopping for alternatives on the results of the product. What will they advantage from it and the manner will it benefit them? Generally, they'll be sensible, so knowledge the technological know-how inside the returned of the object can are also to be had on hand whilst selling to this kind of persona.

Blue humans are probable the very great organization to sell to. As prolonged as you hook up with blues and come to be their friends, they will in reality make the acquisition. To in addition the marketer's powers of persuasion, they are able to add language that compliments the consumer, for instance: "this can sincerely compliment the shade of your eyes" and so on. Others also can upload phrases of endearment to the pitch to in addition the friendship or relationship they're forming in the manner of selling.

Reds are leaders, exuding electricity and self belief. To persuade them to make a purchase, marketers will have to compare them to their pals. Reds are alternatively aggressive thru nature and they in no way need to be outdone thru every person. Saying such things as "your next door neighbor in truth provided 3 of these" triggers their want to shop for the identical quantity of the product being supplied, or extra.

If you're able to exercising the person kinds and suit them to their corresponding shades at the manner to purpose them, simply as slick advertising and marketing and advertising does, you're on to a super element. This capability will proper away provide you with a head start over humans who've no know-how of these man or woman sorts and their behaviors. Having belief into who they may be, even though the affect is best standard, offers you wished records you may draw on.

The Power of Emotions

Emotions are powerful matters. This is an detail of humanity that motivates a whole lot of human behavior, compelling us to behave in wonderful techniques. Therefore, if you could bring about a certain emotion in a person, he can typically remember variety upon to act from that emotion. One properly instance is how you could hire guilt to make someone be extra considerate within the route of you.

Conflicts at artwork are a first rate example. Having a fight with the boss can be destructive on your profession and also have a terrible impact on fashionable place of work dynamics. You have to even lose your system! But if you have a few perception into what makes your boss tick, you have a much better danger of saving your venture and your dating with him.

The top judgment in that is pretty easy. Following the argument, if you keep to behave as even though you have been right all alongside and overtly specific your resentment towards your superior, the horrible feelings springing up can be the present that keeps on giving. And so long as this negativity persists, irrational acts which includes firing you may grow to be the quit result. However, if you technique your boss and permit him apprehend that the conflict became annoying to you and which you regret your element in it, he can also furthermore can be more kindly disposed in the direction of you. He can also additionally be left feeling a hint accountable. After all, he's the individual in the end answerable for the first-rate of the place of job surroundings and the relationships in it. How well you understand your boss will let you apprehend how top notch to navigate the struggle and pop out on top.

There are five emotions which can serve you, as you looking for to gain better manipulate of your relationships and the people you're in them with. Let's compare them:

Fear
This is awesome employed while aggression is displayed in the direction of you. No be counted how huge the other guy is, so long as you function your frame in a way that exudes dominance, the alternative birthday party may additionally moreover rethink taking competitive movement and back off. If you respond with fear, however, expect to be overwhelmed.

They say dogs can fragrance worry on human beings and that giving in it to it within the face of an competitive dog makes the animal far much more likely to act on its competitive instincts.

People aren't that amazing.

If you reply to aggression with the resource of cowering, you're signaling the aggressor's victory. If you respond by status your ground, talking and maintaining your self expectantly, it's no longer going the aggressor will observe thru. Straighten up. Steady your gaze. Place your arms on your hips and face the alternative birthday celebration squarely. Speak in a low, even tone. Just as you may with a canine that's out of place manipulate, you are taking manage again even as you don't give in to the fear of a human aggressor.

Guilt
When human beings get irritated, they act out. If you've gotten someone in a country, they'll commonly reply with both open aggression inside the shape of language or maybe get physical. Sometimes, even though, they'll close down and provide you with the silent treatment. If, but, if you can in some way

redesign their anger into guilt, you may defuse the scenario. This works on your choice. Anger is a bad and negative emotion that if now not rapidly treated can purpose harm now not simplest to you, however to the angry individual and the surroundings the anger is being acted out in. Most human beings will regret having lost their temper in some unspecified time in the destiny and enjoy accountable about it. That guilt is a manner of moving into the person's head and convincing them that outbursts aren't a way of life. You may be the agent of change for a person with anger troubles to learn how to control their outbursts through making them recognize that the guilt they enjoy is justified. It's no longer a nice emotion and those don't care to enjoy it. It can work within the path of enhancing unwelcome behaviors, despite the fact that.

Even if you're the deliver of the anger, you can defuse its outfall in the ones round you through rationally speaking thru the hassle with the person in question. Calmness and reason can do wonders for someone in a kingdom of anger or rage. Sometimes, it manner disposing of the character from the state of affairs they've out of place their mood in and bringing up that they're doing themselves extra damage than top. But reinforcing their enjoy of getting the right of manner in anything dispute they have been in is probably your outstanding bet.

People need to be proper, despite the fact that they aren't. And although it's not right, you may inform Mr. Or Ms. Angry that they'll be. Feeling vindicated will circulate a long manner to shutting down spiraling anger and the negativity which could go with the flow from incidents round it. Convincing the irritated man or woman that they're right is manipulative, however it's going to speak them off the ledge.

Ego
Latching right away to ego is normally recommended in certain situations. For example, in case you find out your marriage is starting to crumble, then overtly telling your partner that others have requested you in case you're experiencing marital troubles need to nip the hassle within the bud. The natural reaction of your accomplice might be to paintings tough to reveal your friends incorrect. This also can artwork with human beings you recognize are doing subjects that they wouldn't care to be criticized for, as their ego drives a number of their behavior.

Addiction

Addiction is going a long way past drugs. Addictive personalities engage in serial sports activities much like the abuse of sex, alcohol, eating, or gambling. They also can turn out to be hooked on extraordinary human beings and being in love with them. When you choose out an addictive person in someone you're inquisitive about, it could be feasible to get them addicted to, in case you realise how to press their buttons.

It's a large step to take, because of the truth having a person addicted to you manner they gained't be able to cope if you go away, so you need to be very positive about what you're getting yourself into. Many humans do it for the incorrect reasons. You also can have discovered whole emotional dependency in a number of the couples you realize. They can barely stand be to apart from each other. That's addiction, no longer love, in maximum times.

Anger

Anger may be very beneficial in the case of someone you apprehend who's being abused. In an abusive state of affairs, the abused companion in the long run loses the need to fight again. Even human beings whose rights are being abused may be reluctant to take action, believing they're powerless. In both scenario, you may help, by way of way of guidance the abused character toward their non-public repressed anger and pushing them to channel it into resistance.

Reading the Signals People Send with Their Bodies

Most of the time, frame language will play a extra big feature in controlling other human beings's minds than the phrases you're pronouncing. It's advocated that during case you're going to take thoughts control considerably, you recognize a bit extra approximately body language than we've already touched on.

Neuro-Linguistic Programming is a arguable technique advanced inside the Seventies with the useful resource of Richard Bandler (a completely shady person) and John Grinder. NLP changed into based totally totally on keen and near assertion of dreams, listening to high-quality micro info distinct body language professionals paid little interest to. Dedicated to controlling people's minds via the subtle use of language, NLP isn't always to be trifled with.

It's a relative of hypnosis and can and has been used for less than noble features.

NLP majors within the minors, particularly tracking the diffused modifications in pores and skin reactions (blushing), eye actions and pupil dilation and private tics, like blinking and 1/2 of-smiles. By taking noting of these micro statistics, Bandler and Grinder decided they'll decide some primary truths about goals thru careful evaluation.

They placed that the ones indicators ought to decide whether or no longer the man or woman have grow to be lying to them, how they processed facts (observed out with the aid of way of eye moves) and their dominant enjoy (sight, listening to, touch, smell, flavor), as well as whether or not the goal became right-brained or left-brained.

The 2nd segment of NLP attracts on the assessment of bodily indicators to arrive on the method of reproducing them, or feeding them once more to the problem. This become blended with language intentionally used to attraction to the purpose's dominant enjoy, as decided through tier one of the NLP way. To mimic a dominant visible revel in, the NLP agent have to rent visible metaphors in his language, for example "I see your element".

By acting a shape of mimicry primarily based definitely on the target's physical clues, the agent should set up rapport via deliberately identifying with the reason's dominant experience, consequently installing recall. The gadget is deepened via manner of using the agent's mimicry of the purpose's body language.

This gadget of conditioning is sealed with the resource of techniques – "eliciting" and "anchoring". Through the same linguistic sleight of hand, the NLP agent is able to draw from the motive an emotional response based at the center experience. For example, odor. Once this reaction has been obtained, the NLP agent pointedly makes physical touch in the identical way every person should at the same time as engaged in a collegial verbal exchange. This might be a slap on the back. In so doing, the emotion the agent has elicited is anchored inside the aim. In principle, if the agent has completed his way well, the same reaction can be elicited every time the agent repeats the act of bodily contact (slap on the again).

Whether mind manipulate is right or lousy, it may't be denied that everybody makes use of it in a single manner or some different. Even in its most effective form, the reason to exchange a person's emotional us of a is there. However, at the same time as used to absolutely exchange the identity of a person -- to mildew his values and ideals to 3 element other than what they typically are -- then it becomes some thing detrimental.

What's essential right here is that you are given an concept about how humans accomplish thoughts manage. Once you're located in a situation in which a person is trying to manipulate you, you'll be aware of what's taking area and no longer the harmless victim of a manipulator. You'll be aware about the techniques manipulators use to get you under their manage and acting in a manner in that you commonly wouldn't act. As outlined above, human beings using NLP are in particular risky and their mimicry is effects recognized. Watch for individuals who over praise, echo your spoken or body language, or appear overly eager to cement your friendship with them.

Mind manipulate doesn't need to be a bad issue, but it's miles constantly manipulative, because of the truth you're using your understanding of some exceptional character to attain a specific result in your interactions with them. Even if the forestall consequences you're looking for is the forestall of an dependancy or defusing a unstable scenario, you are although engaged in an act of manipulation. The horrible connotations related to this word have taken on epic proportions, but manipulation also can be used to diplomatic ends. Ask any profession diplomat, or expert flesh presser and they may allow you to understand that worldwide participants of the own family includes a fantastic deal of technique. They will tell you that to get your law exceeded to keep your guarantees to your elements, you have were given to interrupt a few eggs alongside the manner.

House of Cards' Frank Underwood is a have a observe in manipulation (and nearly constantly for nefarious capabilities). As a politician, even though, he's privy to which way the wind blows. He is aware the motivations of these round them and the manner to leverage their strengths and weaknesses. Who's a friend and who's an enemy? He acts consequently thru retaining his friends close to and his enemies? Even closer.

It's hoped that by the time you've have a look at via this ebook, you'll have at least a number of Frank Underwood's perception and strategic capability (without the evil).

Chapter 5: How To Be Deceptive?

Deception can nice be defined as the artwork of concealing your real intentions and artfully providing them as what human beings may need to decide on they be. It is a mental masquerade in which human beings are capable of actively painting some aspect untrue, whilst hiding the real issue in the decrease lower back of lies and half of-truths. This financial ruin is devoted to taking walks you thru the subtle artwork of deception, its various paperwork and a few tool you'll want to understand it and use it for your gain.

The first requirement of a a hit deception is that of concealing the truth (or at the least part of it). This 'some factor' might be a hard fact or state of affairs that might give up end result into your suffering a loss.

You can perform the number one important of 'hiding' thru severa approach. It might be carried out via your silence (omission) or via turning the attention of these you're trying to misinform towards a few factor else (distraction). You can 'disguise' some thing thru protecting it up with stories, lies, a change of subjects and the presentation of different, greater essential records. However, if you're going to be profligate inside the art of deception, you need to persuade clean of outright mendacity, as lying can be damaging for your reputation if detected. There are higher strategies of doing things.

How to Conceal?
You cowl what you fear will negatively impact you. Naturally, some thing it's far which you are approximately to cover, has the capability to reason you some kind of loss or struggling. You don't need it to be a part of the speak, so you every live silent approximately it, or hide in certainly one of a kind techniques.

Concealing information can be finished in plenty of methods. To begin with, it could be carried out thru actually retaining off the situation of communique. Let's assume you were using the relaxation room at a party in a friend's home and through threat broke a valuable piece of pottery in their vacationer toilet. In order to cover the unlucky incident, you may take subjects on your very very very own palms and weave a tale about the mishap, saying it have become damaged whilst you went within the relaxation room and also you favored your host to understand. You might also choose up the damaged portions of the pottery and cover them somewhere. You should even say you heard it breaking on the identical time as the subsequent tourist went within the relaxation room, but that wouldn't be very wearing, would not it?

The 2d requirement of an effective deception is presenting fiction as truth. Here comes the maximum exciting thing of deception.

Do now not Lie; Tell Half-Truths

In order to advantage a a success deception, it's now not sufficient to genuinely hide a few issue you don't desire to be discovered. The next step seals the deal, because it ensures which you've efficiently prevented detection of what it's far you're looking for to hide or even that you're looking to conceal a few element in any respect.

There's something very vital you need to consider approximately deception. It is not synonymous with mendacity. Lying is pronouncing belongings you apprehend aren't real with a right away face, on the identical time as deception may be practiced for brought noble features. Someone who is aware of that there's a splendid line between truths and half of-truths can appreciate the distinction among mendacity and deception. Let's bear in mind an instance to recognize the idea better.

You're at a night meal thrown through the usage of your boss. The gathering is to have amusing your merchandising. In the temper for a few fun, you make a decision to exceed your drinking functionality and feature greater wine than you normally ought to. Your boss offers to location you up for the night time at his region, as you're nicely over the prison limit to strain home. Although no longer some thing sexual occurs between you and your boss, no longer returning domestic in your associate has created some issue of a sticky state of affairs. This is the shape of state of affairs in which you could use a weapon or from deception's arsenal.

In the example of the cited situation, the desire is that you smooth the air with you companion and reassure her. Nothing negative approximately that proper? You need to inform the reality in case your associate is open to paying attention to it, however if your companion is in reality now not going to swallow the fact, bending it a hint to hold the peace isn't a horrible idea. Say you slept for your automobile due to the fact you have been over the criminal limit and desired to avoid a DUI, or wrapping your automobile round a tree.

You will no longer handiest keep away from an ugly combat. You will see that your associate is grateful to appearance you live through a few other night time and are to be had home alive.

See how that works?
The Deception Tool-Box
Let's learn how to use deception in our every day lives, and extra importantly, learn how to adapt and trade ourselves so that you can be capable of lease the artwork of deception to get out of sticky conditions. It's constantly on hand to understand the way to do that, even though in well-known, sticking with the reality is constantly going to be the super preference. Sometimes, you are confronted with situations

in which deception can hold the day, as in fact as any superhero.

Develop a dynamic persona (or some aspect that looks like one)

The first element people take a look at whilst you stroll right right into a room is your individual. Your character is like an unwritten resume. It determines who humans apprehend you and the manner you'll be treated, at least on the outset.

A dynamic individual is beneficial whilst running toward the artwork of deception, because of the fact that dynamism is instrumental in making sure that human beings's first effect of you is attractive. A nicely set up first have an effect on can do wonders if you are searching forward to giving everyone within the room a great effect for you to placed them in your corner.

Wear clean garments, arise straight away, located a smile to your face and be impeccably dressed. Speak hopefully and make eye touch with all and sundry you communicate to. Your public presentation is a calling card and it ought to be telling people you're assured and comfortable in social situations. If you don't appear to be the type of character who's shady or misleading, people will now not anticipate deception. A lot is primarily based mostly on what people see and what they understand from what they see. What they see have to be faultless presentation that broadcasts "I'm a person you need to apprehend".

Appeal to Everyone
It isn't humanly possible to pleasure without a doubt every body. However, it isn't that difficult to learn how to take no excessive positions in the course of a communication, specially regarding a debatable task. Your intention is to enchantment to absolutely absolutely everyone in the room. You cannot even consider deciding on a selected aspect or starting a debate, or worse, an trouble. Always balance your perspectives and provide pointers at the identical time as speaking about an issue. However, when you have already decided on a factor, persist with it and do now not beneath any times, deviate from it. Make wonderful you do not come to be arguing an excessive amount of to your component. Try to mitigate arguments whenever they erupt in a discourse. Make a funny tale. Offer every body a drink. Be the existence of the birthday party.

Some people have a herbal aptitude for social interactions. They are the folks that don't make ripples, however assist smooth them out. They are those who aren't impolite and who understand a way to technique humans of all ages and be preferred via them. Kids love them. Grandparents approve of them and the common Joe goals he may also need to emulate them.

Humor

No one likes being hit over the top with an opinion. Add a piece of intrigue to your views with the beneficial useful resource of talking in innuendos, and well-timed jokes. If you don't want in reality all of us to be irritated through your perspectives, you may try defensive up the complete problem underneath dialogue with distractions. Change the difficulty. Point and yell "Squirrel!" Just avoid the dialogue. Make jokes to accompany your statements. People love to appearance a likely explosive issue rendered lots less threatening through using humor. It's like letting the air out of a balloon proper in advance than it pops and everybody jumps out of their pores and pores and skin! Instead of becoming angry, they turn out to be guffawing. This is a amazing manner to make sure that you assert your self and appeal to absolutely everyone on the same time.

Chapter 6: Influence– How To Become A Master At It.

All oldsters want our views and evaluations to no longer absolutely be usual however moreover preferred. However, it's not continuously that the people spherical us take them as severely as we might like. Do you locate your self being sidelined and neglected in conversations and lifestyles in wellknown? Does a few thing that comes out of your mouth hold greater cost whilst said thru others inside the equal way you likely did? If you answered "yes" to the ones questions, you can need a couple of pointers.

Welcome to the subsequent economic ruin, which revolves round coaching you a number of the first rate guidelines in the ebook as to the manner to collect your influential power brick through way of brick. As stated above, it's not an easy device. You want to be open to 3 character and behavior hacks, with a view to make your opinions greater influential. Let's begin by using defining what affect is and what fee wielding it has for you.

Influence is the potential to convince others of the veracity and validity of your views. Even higher, have an impact on is having the potential to persuade others to conform collectively with your instance by siding with you. Influence has converted itself from a terrible attribute to a device for survival. Poems and memories may painting the word as some thing unwanted however in the real global, impact is as essential for your survival as water. Influence is better than electricity. Influence is the real strength, in the back of the throne. It may be visible in the corporate power at the coronary coronary heart of American democracy, for example. This is an unsavory instance of impact. Another, more noble instance is probably Pope Francis's effect on worldwide affairs regarding the terrible and climate trade. He is the usage of his strength to steer the opinion of Catholics anywhere inside the international.

If you don't have a say in the society you stay in, you feel your reviews don't recollect; even that your presence in that society doesn't rely. Sometimes, your workplace will name for that you have enough have an effect on to make people be aware of you. When you keep impact, it's no longer much like maintaining electricity. It's now not exercised. It's ambient. People will work in step with your imaginative and prescient of the way topics need to spread. The truth that you keep have an impact on is its very own save you and praise. Your romantic prospects increase ten-fold while you stumble upon as a person who wields affect. Your boss notices your control characteristics, because of the truth you are someone one-of-a-type human beings be aware about and turn to for a have a have a look at of any given state of affairs. Your opinion topics.

If you don't have a energy, begin walking on towards having it. Develop your confidence, initiate connections, do people favors. Do anything it takes to get to the vicinity at which people price your attitude. It offers you clout and whilst humans have clout, others be aware about them and are persuaded through them. Would you concentrate to a person you didn't apprehend? Would you concentrate to a person that everyone else dismisses? Chances are you will not, and that's wherein affect comes into its non-public. Influence presents you with stature to your place of business, your home and your social circle and it permits you to persuade others inside the course of your goals.

What are the benefits of have an effect on?

➢ It receives your interest achieved quicker and smarter. There are many things so that you may be completed mechanically, simply due to the fact you are critical and very own enough have an impact on. When you assert, "jump", people ask "how immoderate?" and that means you have got were given were given sufficient clout to persuade others. That subjects if you want to use deception. People need to have a cause to accept as genuine with in you.

➢ It saves you time and electricity doing art work that can be carried out in higher, more effective approaches. Imagine the time you can keep through selecting to grin in desire to frowning. Find out how thousands greater fast humans cooperate with you when they decide upon you and bear in mind your judgment.

➢ It increases your profile and complements your popularity earlier than individuals who count number to you. A person with effect is reliable. Believe it. If you have got have been given have an impact on, you could use deception any time you want to get what you need, if you recognise a way to apply it appropriately. Again, there's no need to lie and it's no longer encouraged. Bend the reality. Tell human beings first-class what they want to realize. When you're trusted, this will assist get the venture accomplished, no man or woman gets harm and your impact will pay off.

➢ Influence wins you opt for. Anyone with sufficient have an impact on is someone people would like to befriend and comfortable as heaps as. An influential person typically gets some of favors from those who would really like to gain from his have an effect on. You see this effect every day in organization and politics. There are folks that flip heads and function quite some hangers on looking to paintings with them. If you are influential, it's much less complicated to apply deception as a tool to get more from others than they'll be inclined to provide without that effect

The most common social situation is a group. Our lives are full of group conversations that occur in all sectors of them. Whether inside the workplace or our nearby bar, institution conversations are gift possibilities to assemble effect via a assured presentation of your critiques with regards to the communication the enterprise is having. When you end up influential, your enter is sought out. People ask what you observed. However, it's far frequently hard to face your ground, now not to say have a say in a hard and rapid setting. There are generally one or dominant voices. Why shouldn't yours be really one of them? But there are techniques to mitigate the effect of being talked over, or now not sought out in organization communication. Let's communicate about them.

How to Have your Say in Group Conversations
It's normally steady to mention that folks who begin a verbal exchange also are the ones members pay attention to the least. Conversations related to extra than human beings have a specific sample they observe. The one starting the communique generally wishes to speak approximately considerable subjects of little effect. The person speaking right away after the initiator follow up their contributions to the mission and their opinions. It's people who communicate following those introductory monologues who're expected to carry a few aspect current or super into the communication. The art work of group communication dictates that you need to look ahead to your turn or keep away from speaking until the immediate seems too opportune to skip up. When that second arrives, you want to select out your phrases cautiously so that you cannot end up offending all people inside the

commercial enterprise corporation. Be clever, be witty, but be applicable to what's being said. If you waft off hassle remember wide variety, then you could now not get the goal marketplace on your aspect. The complete point is that you want to steer the communication, so make your words rely.

Remember, you are there to persuade others to definitely receive your views. There is a specific manner in that you want to continue to make certain this impact. Here are a few recommendations to so-

➢ Start off with the aid of manner of thanking people who spoke in advance than you. It is a simple sign of gratitude that lays the muse of your first have an effect on. By thanking them, you are suggesting that their contributions were nicely received and preferred by way of way of the usage of you, which is a great sign and suggests courtesy.

➢ Do not start attacking special perspectives provided, regardless of your preference to obtain this. Be conciliatory and and ask why they selected to say what they said. Do not factor out the holes of their particular judgment. Don't parse their terms. Do no longer placed a duration in your comments. Let people digest them and turn out to be curious about your quit. The thing is to growth your have an effect on thru manner of effectively decreasing a person else's who's influential in the company worried. By being courteous and now not too eager to criticize, your stock rises. You acquired't get any brownie elements for being rude or looking to humiliate the opposite birthday celebration with sarcasm or snideness. Regardless of the manner lots better your argument is, don't be a smartass about it.

➢ Having with politeness made your case, you're now organized to lay down your very personal views decisively. Remember that with the aid of now, the institution you're in communique with is hoping you're saying a few component they can latch right now to. Be prepared. Be sure of what you're pronouncing and don't provide actually anyone any motive to want to assault you. Maintain a courteous and generous demeanor on the same time as strongly litigating to your point of view.

➢ To tackle the foregoing hypothetical situation, start by means of way of mentioning you're no longer nice in case you're right and also you'd recognize others filling within the blanks. Be self-effacing and humble. Make positive you tell each person that at instances your reviews can be a hint vague and that, once in a while, you annoy even yourself. No one inside the business enterprise will revel in right approximately having a circulate at someone of such humility. Whether you're feeling humble or now not, a said humility will constantly advantage you wanted have an effect on and get people in your factor. This is a conventional method used inside the political global, wherein the "log cabin fable" (humble origins) is a prized political device.

➢ The closing stage of a collection communique on the identical time as you may sit up for all people agreeing together in conjunction with your perspectives at the subject at hand. Effective, influential speaking isn't the act of doling out phrases at random. It is the art work of information what to mention and when. It moreover includes know-how what no longer to mention. Keep in mind the following elements while concerned in a hard and fast talk:

➢ Politeness doesn't damage truly absolutely everyone. A little little little bit of politeness may likely honestly sway others on your pick. If you're impolite or abrasive, people won't see you in as influential a slight it's miles the final problem you need. Sometimes you can control a communication because of your politeness as no man or woman can object to it.

➤ Be concise. A modern have a have a look at located out that sentences simplest five phrases lengthy have more impact than sentences of any other length.

Try the subsequent workout-
A. Knowledge brings the bearer power.
B. Knowledge is strength.

Please be aware that the a good deal much less phrases in a sentence, the greater impact it has. The sort of terms in a sentence works either in its want or closer to it. It has been effectively set up that once people use fewer phrases of their spoken sentences, they have got extra intellectual effect than people who use extra.

Everyone loves it even as records is summed up in the most inexperienced way feasible. Concise and abridged sorts of information aren't in reality smooth to digest, but moreover constitute an art work form. It's not smooth to craft concise messages. If you are capable of explicit extra with using just a few words, you're adept at bring your mind with minimal property and try. This trait in a person is exemplary and one which regularly leads others to trust that individual is a person virtually truly well worth listening to. Someone able to deliver records correctly might be heard and this is the concept of have an impact on.

As mentioned earlier on this e-book, have an effect on isn't always synonymous with instilling fear in others. Fear is a byproduct of strength, no longer have an impact on. Here is a state of affairs that will help you recognize the difference among influencing and instilling worry-

James is the boss of your place of job. You are his right hand who receives most of the roles carried out. Though he officially manages the department, you are the only doing all of the grimy artwork. People listen to you extra than they pay attention to James. In a business organisation audit, a particular document is placed to comprise a few sensitive statistics that have to in no way had been positioned in it. The pastime of rooting out the organisation rat starts offevolved offevolved, with James main the search. The rat is determined seeking to shred the proof by a colleague. This colleague comes to inform you, as you've got were given grow to be a primary influencer within the place of business.

Normally, this colleague may want to have approached institution lead, James. But James isn't always well-preferred and is truely not as influential as you're and isn't always depended on through many within the place of work. So the colleague recognizes your superior "slight" reputation and is derived to you. He trusts you and your opinions.

The distinction among having impact and instilling fear is that have an effect on requires no actual electricity or authority. Power is what it's far with the resource of manner of respectable declaration. Influence is unofficial and consequently, subversive. It can recuperation problems energy can't. It can get records energy can't and it can have its ear to the ground in a manner energy can't, due to the take transport of as true with an influencer enjoys among pals. You want to apprehend that being an influential man or woman does no longer suggest you're a person to be feared. You're a peer with mainly appealing traits. You are approachable and friendly. A high-quality demeanor is useful, but humor doubles your role and consequently, your impact. Learn to snicker with human beings, no longer at them. To be someone of have an effect on, you want to be a humans individual and on their degree – in no way speakme down, or retaining yourself above your colleagues. People will consider you to maintain the day once they have dedicated their share of errors. You are the answer to the "Jameses" of this world, who don't manage humans nicely and don't apprehend the way to be influential of their private areas of exertions. You recognize a way to try this.

Another thing that lets in advantage buddies and feature an impact on humans is in no way being afraid to admit you made a mistake. Laughing at yourself is a top notch manner to advantage recognize, because of the truth dad and mom which may be capable of do this are also able to be greater information on the same time as others make mistakes.

Leadership is frequently considered identical to proudly owning have an impact on, and that's simply so. Whether you lead from the the front, center, or from in the lower back of, human beings admire you. You come upon as someone who cannot most effective lead however also even as situations call for it of you, you may go into reverse and make the tough decisions. Remember, manipulate isn't about being the boss. A boss directs humans to do the art work while a leader works alongside together with his people, influencing them to offer their brilliant art work.

In nowadays's international of lies and deceit, it's critical you have got got have been given a few playing playing cards up your sleeve. Influence receives you friends and collaborators and wins you choose. When you have impact, you're pretty likely to triumph and ultimately, lead from the nook place of work. It isn't a horrible detail to have your way, because of the reality no person is going to do it for. No one is going to look when you, except you. When you understand the way to wield effect to move on at the facet of your life and help others, you may have discovered out a critical survival potential and one which lets in you to take you via plenty more without a trouble than in case you didn't have it.

Be the individual that affects others. Be the pass-to person and you could use notion and thoughts manipulate to compel situations to unfold within the way you want them to. People will receive as true with you. If you want to apply a touch little bit of deception on occasion, it is going to be omitted or no longer even suspected because it doesn't go along with the picture of you that human beings see. They received't see the machinations, the maneuvering, or the strategic sleight of hand you're so deftly using, underneath the table. They'll certainly see the results your impact is able to generating and that's what ultimately topics.

Chapter 7: Tool-Kit For Persuasion

Welcome to the economic wreck of this e-book that's certain that will help you win at lifestyles. Not each one parents is adept at making others see our problem of view. At instances the need for it becomes so vital we find out ourselves clutching at straws, searching out the right way to make our factor. This monetary damage has been especially written to equip you to recognize your proper persuasive capability. It's primarily based completely totally on business enterprise models and moreover on models in non-public relationships, as the ones were showed powerful as regards to the first-rate art work of persuasion.

Seem Confident

It doesn't count number whether or not or now not you accept as true with what you're announcing or not. Neither does it depend whether or not or not you are actually extremely good about your factor of view's credibility. If you need to steer others to honestly accept your opinion, step one is to be unwaveringly assured. If you look and sound like a person who has studied all of the components and done all his studies inside the query below talk, humans are sure to as a minimum be privy to you and, more importantly, accept as true with you. Self-self guarantee solves at least half the problem. The rest can be done via following the hints in this financial disaster.

Confidence doesn't mean being a clever ass. It doesn't advocate conceitedness, each. People have little apprehend for folks who seem to deem themselves superior to others and whose attitude is condescending. Make your statistics enlightening and supply it, no longer from above, however laterally. Arrogant human beings are lots much less probably to get the effects they need due to the truth they speak all the manner all of the way all the way down to people and take transport of as actual with themselves to be beyond reproach. Confident people are humble enough to understand once they're wrong and are continuously ready to admit it.

It's profitable searching people to apprehend the difference and if you try this in a public region and see how people engage with each distinctive, you could be conscious that the smart ass holds himself a superb manner. Make be aware of his body language and the manner he expresses his feel of innate superiority.

Resolve not to duplicate this. Confidence manner you receive as actual with your self and that others can believe you and bear in mind me, humans can inform the distinction between that and its dysfunctional cousin, conceitedness.

Do your Research

It's unwise to jump into a persuasive function without doing your homework, regarding primary and concrete data. Know what matters are authentic, hooked up and nicely wellknown. Find the weak spot in the statistics as they stand. Without having first won a thorough know-how of your situation remember wide variety, it's far an unwise desire to walk right right into a communique. By displaying that you have observe about the difficulty or you are acquainted with it thru non-public experience, you benefit the bear in mind of your audience and assure them which you understand what you are talking about. I can offer you with an example proper right here. When visiting a place that I wanted to transport to, and with out even consulting my associate, I determined that the simplest manner of attaining the skip emerge as to have the right solutions to any questions that could get up. I wanted to make my solutions align with the manner of existence my partner located as tremendous. A 365 days in advance than I did this, there has been no manner on earth my companion might likely have considered transferring from one give up of the u . S . A . To the alternative, but due to the reality I changed into able to finesse my presentation and use my private enjoy to influence my associate to reap this, we moved inner six months. I took the movements I did with out letting directly to my partner, who have become immune to the idea of moving, now not believing it became viable. My self belief and capability to offer the right responses to questions asked of me in the favored network, further to a small omission (not telling my partner), opened the door to a cutting-edge lifestyles.

Appeal to Emotions

The golden rule of persuasion is that if you may't convince human beings based on what's authentic, you want to persuade them primarily based on how they feel. It is a regular law that people are pushed with the aid in their emotions. Emotions are as crucial as logical arguments on the subject of persuasive values. If you're faced with the undertaking of convincing someone to go through a number one change, or every unique course of motion, attractive to their feelings may be a critical help in doing so. Emotions are so powerful that they have got shaken empires to their foundations or even modified the essential way subjects are performed. They are common to us all.

While doing all your research, search for viable possibilities to enchantment to the feelings of those listening. People have emotional susceptible spots and some of those are common to us all. Find this spot and hit it difficult. Exploit their emotional ties to a few factor all of them preserve expensive and your phrases can be applauded and frequent. Appeals to patriotism, the own family, justice and further normal topics are nicely-acquired and definitely beneficial in bringing most human beings round to your way of questioning.

Television advertisements do that every one of the time. By analyzing social norms in goal demographics, advertising and marketing companies are capable of pinpoint their marketplace and promote to it. Appeals to emotions can embody images of fluffy kitten cavorting amongst rolls of lavatory paper, or performing lots of antics to promote phone packages for a cable enterprise agency.

111

Also employed are ensures of advanced health in food advertising and marketing. Margarine turned into marketed for years at the promise of low ldl cholesterol and quite much absolutely everyone provided in. Recently, despite the fact that, butter has once more supplanted margarine, this is stated now to be pretty volatile to human fitness. People buy into the message because of the truth they take into account it will solution a hassle or want. People go together with what they need to trust. Telling them what they need to listen, even as strolling toward the sale, is a time-venerated technique of persuasion.

Use Rhetoric

Rhetoric is a device that doesn't solution a question; it asks each other query that nearly solutions the number one. Let me assist you with an instance-

Person A- "Gryffindor is the high-quality house at Hogwarts."

Rhetorical reply- "The others want to be quite redundant homes, I count on?"

When you answer a query with a query, you not nice shake the question-asker's credibility however additionally firmly assert your difficulty. Rhetoric is a super manner to win arguments and persuade those listening. It additionally lets you benefit recognition specifically if used at the same time as someone you are attempting to persuade is listening and getting to know out of your strategies.

Rhetoric moreover is based for your capability to assume efficiently about an difficulty and assume responses for your technique. It's about crafting a powerful and robust message that's resultseasily digested and but elegantly constructed.

Keep Sarcasm to the Minimum
Sarcasm is a lot of a laugh to rent however can positioned people off. You can't anticipate to win over human beings with sarcasm by myself. You must have data and less expensive arguments to your choose too. When you lodge to the everyday use of sarcasm, it may make you seem shady and plenty tons much less assured approximately your real argument. It can also make you seem a bit of a buffoon. It shows a lack of creativity and the desired facts

to win arguments and may torpedo your credibility.

Sarcasm is a type of humor that doesn't suit with severa conditions. If incorrectly or ineptly deployed, it will pleasant come up with a recognition as someone who isn't able to take topics significantly. That's not what you need. Is it? You need to be an influencer and buffoons seldom have a extraordinary deal have an impact on to talk of. Humor is constantly welcome, however resorting to relentless sarcasm may additionally consign you to the feature of buffoon. Be aware of the potential impact a surfeit of sarcasm will ought to your recognition. If you're intense approximately gaining have an effect on in your circle, it's essential which you be aware of any tendency you need to do be overly sarcastic.

Sound Reasonable
Your factor want now not be an inexpensive one. But your arguments need to continuously sound credible. When you need to persuade human beings, you need to hold in thoughts that they have got to enjoy connected to what you're attempting to mention. To set up this connection, you need to begin from a foundation of motive and correct judgment.

Your rhetorical framework should usually be primarily based on these factors. You accumulate this thru sounding less costly. You can not convince human beings to go past their personal barriers in the occasion that they fear that it's risky or volatile to gain this. You want to put them comfortable.

Travel offerings frequently sell excursion desires to humans via making their excursion packages sound very reasonably-priced even to the ones on a confined income. These are often packaged in a manner that led humans to remember they were internal gain, financially. It's regularly the case that the dream and the fact are very one-of-a-type. Often, hidden charges, expenses and taxes now not said up the the front, which made the packages less reasonably-priced – and the proffered dream nicely out of obtain.

Package and message a products or services in a way that speaks to humans's hopes and desires and they'll skip for it. Credit card agencies do that every one the time. It's no longer actual deception, however the entire reality is within the very excellent print that's nearly no longer viable to study, concealed as it is under layers of advertising and marketing.

The astronomical overdue prices charged via the ones businesses, coupled with clean credit make having a credit rating card a mine state of affairs for lots people. The fact is that credit card organizations maintain out clean credit rating that allows you to hit humans with fees, information lots of their clients will fall into catastrophic debt.

I gave those examples because of the reality they show that sounding reasonably-priced elicits a pleasing reaction. The weight loss plan and weight reduction business business enterprise is a few one of a kind instance of talking to people's hopes and dreams, offering a way to a urgent trouble they need solved. Silver bullet solutions to lose weight via the diet regime, pill or powder of the on the spot are everywhere. Do those solutions paintings? Some may work quick, however there may be no silver bullet to weight reduction, as most mother and father recognize. Lifestyle modifications that people regularly determine upon not to pursue are the solution and they call for something of human beings. Most human beings want smooth solutions.

Before and after pix provided as evidence of the weight loss answer's efficacy are carefully curated, however are hardly ever sincere representations of the healthy dietweight-reduction plan, tablet or powder's outcomes at the challenge. Look at the angles and lighting fixtures hired. Look on the stance of the model. It's not hard to look that there may be a positive degree of deception at artwork. While it all appears hopeful at the floor, the reality is that sleight of hand and tips with mirrors are at paintings.

Deception is a part of our lives and snake oil is anywhere. Understanding the manner it's hired no longer fine allows you save you falling prey to it, but will present you with the ability to use its recommendations towards a more a success existence.

Watch Reactions
When you're running towards persuading a person, you could't be overly assertive in urgent your point. Be nice to keep in mind which you're having a verbal exchange. Allow yourself the opportunity and the time to assess people's reactions to what you're saying. Look for any signs and symptoms which you're losing inside the attempt to persuade your project. Rolling the eyes, elevating the eyebrows and crossing the palms are all bodily signs that your message isn't convincing the character you're speaking

to and they feel you understand it. Be fine to read your problem as you determine to persuading him in your factor of view. It's vital that you not be so busy making your aspect which you fail to do that.

Proceed in line with what you examine in front of you. People's reactions will manual you. If the situation appears to be turning off (see above) tweak your message. Try to decide at which thing you began out out losing your scenario and adjust consequently. You might also moreover moreover want to confront the issue and ask why he rolled his eyes/raised his eyebrows/crossed his hands. Confronting the objection forces the problem out into the open and offers you the opportunity to answer it. It also speaks for your willingness to speak.

That said, a few objections can't be spoke back and a few human beings in truth can't be persuaded, no matter how hard you attempt. Choose your battles and recognise who you're talking to. As said in advance on this ebook, some topics are an entire lot higher ready to face as lots because the efforts of a persuasive voice they disagree with. They're not the individuals who interest you.

Subtlety is the Key

Even whilst you're within the right and you're conscious that no argument inside the room have to venture your statements, don't bypass "entire Hulk" on the ones you're talking to. Subtlety is the signal of a exceptional speaker. Work on gaining knowledge of it. Hitting human beings over the top with a wet fish obtained't persuade them of some thing but your aggression. Be affected man or woman. Don't rush. Be a butterfly, not a steamroller. Your language should leave room for talk. Frame it as open for input. People respond to that form of humility.

Suggest. Don't Demand

Persuasion is not about telling others what to do, it's about major them toward a cease. Persuasion is supported with the useful useful resource of logical statements which might be demonstrably supported through facts. Lay out an possibility that makes revel in. Saying you don't like some difficulty, or disagree with some thing is warmth beneficial or fine. Having a practicable possibility is extremely good.

Listening

Listening is sincerely as vital as watching body language. Be wonderful you're paying attention to the message in its totality with the resource of giving your entire hobby. This is one of the most important portions of device you have were given in your deception toolbox. If you don't take time to pay attention to human beings and to look at them, you stroll inside the path of discussions and interactions with them without a doubt blind.

If people assume they had been heard, they will be an lousy lot greater open in your diffused efforts at persuading them inside the route of a few aspect end you're drawing; some factor demand you'd care to make of them. People be given as actual with people who pay attention to them and lead them to simply accept as actual with that their point of view certainly counts for a few aspect.

Observation
Your powers of declaration are as vital to you as your listening abilities. Observation offers you the best perception into the kind of character you're interacting with. Observation allows you realise who you're talking to and whether you may enlist them into your project, your purpose, the mission available, or your conclusions.

Your functionality to find out man or woman kinds is strong. Don't anticipate you can do this with common sense, on my own. Depending on raw instinct can lead you off course. Analysis is the guide you need to correctly decide the shape of man or woman you're speakme to. Learn out of your super observations of frame language and the form of phrases employed, similarly to difficulty subjects that rise up, and your persuasive abilities will enhance incredibly, because of the fact you may pick out your objectives because it want to be and enlist the right first-class friend on every occasion.

These competencies will help you with a view to manipulate and navigate many situations correctly. No, we don't like telling lies and the usage of deception, however once in a while it's miles a vital evil to get things completed. If you use all the equipment that we have given you on this monetary smash, probabilities are you'll no longer handiest be able to gather what you got all the way down to do, but will set an instance to others as to the way to get that finished. People will apprehend your facility with people.

As a remaining tool in the course of the usage of persuasion, it's typically in truth properly worth becoming a member of a debate society, or speaking guild (like Toastmasters). Learning the manner to craft rhetorical strategies to problems and to talk in the the front of various humans is a life expertise in case you want to make you greater assured and effective in lifestyles.

While I was attending university, the speak society grow to be one of the most useful of gadget I had at my disposal. Knowing the way to enhance problems and characteristic an impact at the critiques of others changed right right into a superb self guarantee builder. This knowledge labored towards making me extra influential in my peer organization and assisted me in moving earlier in lifestyles, in my interactions with human beings at work and in social situations.

Insincerity and a lack of conviction are smooth for people to locate. Watch someone talk in public and you can see that those unfortunate traits are almost palpable. To convince those round you, you've got to say what it's miles you have to mention with the maximum conviction. Even in case you recognise that the real basis for what you're saying is risky, you may persuade yourself of the proposition's usefulness by means of constructing the argument. Politicians try this all of the time. The human beings in the ancient past craft messages around insurance which inform human beings the maximum conceivable and easy to digest tale across the coverage they're speaking about. They won't even just like the coverage. That doesn't recall. Via the manipulation of the message, they are allow to deliver it with conviction, as they've arrived at an reputation due its processing as a public message. It is now digestible and they're able to stay with that. And you can do the equal. By constructing a rhetorical framework which allows unpleasant, or hard to digest messages this is available, you come to be the bearer of a message you – and your listeners – can life with. In this way, each phrase you're announcing can be rock strong and heard as such. There may be no question of your sincerity.

When you are capable of produce results like that, then you switch out to be a superb persuader, much like any pro flesh presser. By internalizing your message, you benefit the potential to bypass it on as a powerful and compelling messenger. People don't shoot powerful messengers, because the message has been massaged right right into a palatable product that appeals.

Chapter 8: Types Of Mind Control

• The concept of mind manage has been round for many years now. People have had every fascination and worry of what would possibly rise up if a person in which able to control their minds and motive them to do subjects in competition to their will.

• Conspiracy theories run abound approximately authorities officers and one-of-a-kind humans of energy using their competencies to control what small organizations of human beings are doing.

• Even a few court docket docket times had been added up the usage of the excuse of brainwashing as an cause in the back of why they dedicated the crime they may be accused of. Despite the dramatization of mind manipulate that has been portrayed in the media and the movies, there can be little this is identified about the first-rate forms of thoughts manage and the way each of them paintings. This bankruptcy

• will discover a bit bit approximately the most common kinds of mind manage as an introduction to explaining extra about this thrilling subject matter.

• While there are many specific forms of thoughts manage that can be used to
• manipulate the meant sufferer, there are 5 which is probably most normally perception of. These embody brainwashing, hypnosis, manipulation, persuasion, and deception. These will all be discussed underneath.

• Brainwashing Brainwashing is the primary type of mind manipulate to speak about. Brainwashing is basically the technique in which someone might be connived to abandon ideals that that they'd in the beyond on the way to take new beliefs and values. There are pretty some approaches that this can be completed however the fact that not all of them could be taken into consideration awful.
• For instance, if you are from an African u.S.A. And then skip to America, you will frequently be pressured to exchange your values and ideals an excellent manner to healthy in
• with the brand new culture and surroundings which you are in. On the other hand, the ones in interest camps or when a present day dictator government is taking on, they'll regularly go through the method of brainwashing in order to
• persuade citizens to take a look at along peacefully.

• Many humans have misconceptions of what brainwashing is. Some humans have more paranoid thoughts about the exercise which include thoughts control gadgets which are sponsored via using the government and which might be belief to be easily turned on like a remote control. On the opposite component of things, there are

• skeptics who do now not believe that brainwashing is possible the least bit and that

• anyone who claims it has happened is mendacity. For the most thing, the exercise of brainwashing will land somewhere within the center of those thoughts.

• During the workout of brainwashing, the trouble is probably happy to

• alternate their ideals about some thing thru a combination of different methods. There is not sincerely one approach that can be used within the path of this system so it may be hard to place the exercise proper proper into a neat little discipline. For the maximum element, the hassle could be separated from all the topics that they understand.

• From there, they'll be broken down into an emotional state that makes them inclined earlier than the today's ideas are introduced. As the trouble absorbs this new data, they'll be rewarded for expressing thoughts

127

• and mind which go together with those new ideas. The profitable is what's going to be used if you want to red meat up the brainwashing that is taking place.

• Brainwashing isn't always some issue that is new to society. People had been using those strategies for a long term. For instance, in a historic context, humans who've been prisoners of wars have been regularly broken down earlier than being persuaded to adjustments factors. Some of the maximum a success times of those

• may want to bring about the prisoner becoming a very fervent convert to the modern-day component. These practices had been very new in the starting and will frequently be enforced relying on who've come to be in price. Over time, the term of

• brainwashing become advanced and some more techniques have been brought an great manner to make the exercising extra commonplace. The extra present day techniques ought to depend upon the field of psychology considering masses of these thoughts have been used to illustrate how people may trade

their minds via persuasion.

There are many steps that go with the brainwashing manner. It is not a few thing that is going to just take region to you whilst you stroll down the

avenue and communicate to someone that you have just met. First off, one of the maximum critical necessities that consist of brainwashing being a achievement is that the issue have to be saved in isolation the undertaking is able to be spherical different people and influences, they'll discover ways to think as an man or woman and the brainwashing will not be powerful in any respect. Once the undertaking is in isolation, they will go through a way that is supposed to interrupt down their private self. They are advised that all the topics they understand are faux and are made to revel in like the entirety they do is inaccurate. After months of going thru all of this, the difficulty will experience like they are terrible and the guilt goes to overwhelm them.

1. Once they have got reached this point, the agent will start to lead them closer to the brand new notion device and identification that

2. Is desired. The trouble can be delivered about believe that the contemporary selections are all their non-public and so it is more likely to stick.

three. The whole approach of brainwashing can take many months to even years. It isn't always some aspect this is going to reveal up in handiest a communication and for the maximum factor it's going to not be able to display up outside of prison camps and some remoted instances. Chapter 2 will circulate into greater element of what occurs all through the 3 essential levels of brainwashing and the way the entire system takes location.

4. For the most component, folks who undergo brainwashing have accomplished so while a person is honestly trying to influence them of a modern element of view. For

five. Instance, if you are in an issue with a chum and that they convince you that their mind make feel, you've got technically lengthy past via brainwashing.

6. Sure, it can not be evil and also you have been capable of reflect onconsideration on it all logically, however you have got got been but satisfied to change the beliefs which you held before. It can be very uncommon that a person undergoes real brainwashing wherein they'll have their whole fee device modified. It will commonly get up in the course of the technique of coming round to a ultra-cutting-edge component of view, no matter whether or now

not the techniques used were forcible or no longer.
Hypnosis

The subsequent shape of thoughts manage this is well-known is hypnosis. There are pretty a few special definitions of what hypnosis is. According to the American Psychological Association, hypnosis is a cooperative interplay wherein the hypnotist will offer guidelines that the participant will reply to. □

Many human beings have end up familiar with the techniques of hypnosis way to famous performances wherein people are suggested to do ridiculous or unusual responsibilities. Another shape of hypnosis that is gaining in popularity is the sort that makes use of this exercising for its restoration and scientific blessings, specially as regards to the good buy of hysteria and pain. In a few times, hypnosis has been able to reduce dementia symptoms in a few patients. As you may see, there are a number of precise motives that hypnosis that can be used. The point in which it starts offevolved offevolved to grow to be thoughts manipulate is while the hypnotist is capable of propose guidelines that can be unstable or alternate the manner that the participant acts of their surroundings. For most people, after they pay attention approximately hypnosis they do not forget a person on stage who's swinging an eye fixed fixed backward and forward on the way to located the player in a trance. If you have got were given been to a degree show for amusement, you could have a few pics in your head of the ridiculous acts that the members finished. In reality, oldsters which can be going through what's □

taken into consideration actual hypnosis are going thru a method this is very unique from this photo. □

"The hypnotist does not hypnotize the individual. Rather, the hypnotist serves as a shape of educate or show whose process is to help the individual become hypnotized," □

said John Kihlstrom. This way that the hypnotist works to get the participant into an altered usa of mind honestly so they'll be extra open to □
guidelines which might be given.

Many of the folks who undergo hypnosis say that they may be in a sleep-like trance sort of state. Despite the ones mind, even as beneath hypnosis the player is in a rustic that includes bright fantasies, heightened suggestibility, and centered hobby.

This new usa makes them more at risk of the pointers that the hypnotist can be giving to them.

It is hard to element the results that hypnosis can have on subjects because the research will range pretty a piece for anyone who undergoes it. Some topics will file feeling like they are detached from the whole revel in, a few will revel in exceptionally snug at a few degree in the hypnosis, and despite the fact that others will revel in that the movements they may be doing will upward push up outdoor in their conscious options. On the opportunity aspect of factors, people will united states of america of the us that

they may be without a doubt aware of their surroundings and could also be capable of carry out conversations ultimately of their hypnotic nation.

Some experiments which have been finished by means of manner of Ernest Hilgard suggests that hypnosis may be used so you can adjust the perceptions of the topics. The take a look at accomplished thru Hilgard blanketed an training of the problem to now not experience any ache of their arm. After they were knowledgeable this, the undertaking had their arm placed in some ice water.

Those who did this check and have been no longer hypnotized needed to take their fingers out of the water in only some seconds considering that they felt ache. Those who had been hypnotized had been able to leaving their hands within the water for a couple of minutes without experiencing pain.

While greater studies will need to be completed, this check indicates how sturdy mind control may be at the same time as using the technique of hypnosis.

There are many virtually considered one of a kind programs showed through studies that hypnosis may be used for collectively with: Treating persistent pain which includes that determined with rheumatoid arthritis.

Treating and reducing the pain that comes subsequently of
childbirth.

Reducing the symptoms and symptoms which is probably associated with dementia.

Some ADHD sufferers have visible cut charge in their signs and symptoms after the usage of hypnotherapy.

Reducing instances of vomiting and nausea in chemotherapy patients.

Controlling of ache all through dental techniques.

Eliminating and decreasing pores and skin conditions consisting of psoriasis and warts.

Alleviating signs and symptoms which is probably associated with Irritable

Bowel Syndrome.

These are just a few of the makes use of which have end up not unusual with hypnosis.

While many humans are underneath the false impression that the usage of hypnosis is used to control the state of affairs and motive them to perform awful acts or denounce their non-public beliefs, the most common uses are the ones for enhancing the fitness of the people.

Most specialists are in agreement that the effect of hypnosis as a shape of mind manipulate isn't always definitely a reality. While it

may be possible to steer the thoughts to make a few modifications inside the behavior and behavior of the situation, it isn't probably that the hassle will exchange their complete gadget of beliefs clearly through this system. Many of the those who are licensed on this profession will use it to assist the situation in self-development and ache control in location of for trying to take over their minds.

Manipulation Manipulation is some other shape of mind control that can be applied in severa approaches to decide the way the
person will assume. In this guidebook, manipulation will speak with mental manipulation. This is a shape of social have an impact on that works to alternate the behavior or perception of others. This is finished the use of abusive, misleading, and underhanded approaches.

This form of thoughts control is used to enhance the pastimes of the handiest manipulating, frequently on the fee of others. The strategies which might be used are regularly considered misleading, devious, abusive, and exploitative. Many human beings will understand at the identical time as they may be being manipulated or at the same time as others are being manipulated spherical them, but they do not recognize this as a shape of thoughts control. This can often be a hard shape of thoughts control to avoid due to the reality that the manipulation will commonly arise a number of the mission and someone they recognize properly.

Manipulation leaves the priority feeling like they don't have any choice in the take into account.

They will have been cautioned outright lies or 1/2 of of-truths and did no longer recognise the overall amount of the situation till it's far too past due. If they find out about the
situation beforehand of time, the agent is probably capable of blackmail and use the problem if you need to get to the very last goal. The situation essentially turns into stuck due to the fact the agent could have crafted the whole thing out inside the type of manner that they may now not get in hassle, the situation can take the blame or get damage if it consists of that, and the agent will make it to their final intention.
The maximum tough problem approximately this is that the agent is incapable of feeling the desires of their hassle or some different person; they'll be no longer going to care if the priority gets harmed within the approach whether or not or now not it's miles emotional or physical harm. While the state of affairs is probably emotionally invested within the scenario, the

agent can be capable to walk away (so long as they meet their very last cause)

without feeling any remorse or regret at what took place alongside the way. This may be a dangerous form of thoughts manipulate due to the fact the agent goes to be an professional at it, being able to blackmail, threaten, and perform a little element else is critical; at times they'll even be able to expose subjects round so the difficulty looks as if they may be going insane.

Persuasion

Persuasion is every other form of thoughts manage this is much like manipulation in that it truly works in order to influence the behaviors, motivations, intentions,

attitudes, and beliefs of the problem.

There are many super motives that persuasion might be implemented in ordinary life and often it's far a essential shape of communique a great manner to get people of differing mind at the identical page.

For instance, in enterprise, the method of persuasion is probably used if you want to alternate someone's mind-set in the direction of some object, idea, or occasion that is taking region.

During the method, both written or spoken terms may be used in case you need to supply reasoning, feelings, or records to the alternative individual.

Another time that persuasion may be used is to meet a non-public benefit. This could in all likelihood encompass trial advocacy, whilst giving a income pitch, or throughout an election advertising and marketing and marketing advertising marketing campaign. While none of those are considered horrible or evil, they're although utilized in a way to persuade the listener to behave or assume in a quality way. One interpretation of persuasion is that it uses one's positional or personal belongings to alternate the attitudes or behaviors of others. There also are
numerous amazing sorts of persuasion which can be recognized; the approach of
changing the beliefs or attitudes via appeals to cause and not unusual feel is referred to as systematic persuasion; the way wherein beliefs and attitudes are changed due to an attraction to emotions or behavior is referred to as heuristic persuasion.
Persuasion is a shape of mind manipulate that is utilized in society all the time.

When you talk to a person about politics you could strive to influence them to expect the identical manner that you do.

When you are being attentive to a political marketing campaign, you're being persuaded to vote a sure manner. When a person is attempting to sell you a present day product, there is a lot of persuasion that is taking location.

This shape of thoughts control is so famous that maximum humans do no longer even apprehend that it's miles happening to them at all. The difficulty will occur whilst a person takes the time to steer you into believing ideals and values that do not in form up on your very own system of values.

There are a whole lot of great varieties of persuasion which can be to be had. Not all of them have an evil reason, but all of them are going to art work to get the scenario to trade their minds approximately some thing. When a flesh presser comes on television, they'll be seeking to get the mission, or the voter, to vote a positive way at the ballot on election day. When you spot a business on tv or on-line, the

140

organisation who supplied that commercial is making an attempt to get the concern to buy that product. All of those are varieties of persuasion which is probably bent at trying to get the situation to alternate the manner that they anticipate.

Deception

Finally, deception is likewise taken into consideration a form of mind manage due to the effect that it can have on the difficulty.

Deception is used on the way to propagate within the scenario beliefs in sports and subjects that simply are not real, whether they may be entire lies or truely partial lies. Deception can consist of severa diverse things which include sleight of hand, propaganda, and dissimulation, concealment, camouflage, distraction.

This form of mind control is so risky due to the truth the task regularly does now not recognise that any thoughts control is going on in any respect. They had been glad that one element is actual even as the complete opposite is proper. This can get risky while the deceit is hiding facts that might maintain the undertaking stable.

Often, deception is visible inside the path of relationships and will generally result in feelings of distrust and betrayal between the two partners. When deception takes place, there was a contravention of the relational policies and might make it hard for the companion to trust the possibility for a long time. It may be especially destructive because maximum humans are use to trusting those round them, mainly relational partners and friends, and expect them to be honest to them for the maximum aspect. When they find out that a person they may be close to is deceiving them, they will have troubles with trusting others and could not have the feel of safety that they may be used to.

Deception can purpose quite a few issues in a dating or in the agent and trouble. The task could have an entire lot of problems trusting the agent in the destiny when they discover approximately the deception.

There might be instances even as the deception may be achieved with a purpose to assist out the relationship. These may additionally need to include topics collectively with not telling a associate while someone says something advocate approximately them. Other instances the deception is extra spiteful or dangerous in nature which encompass whilst the agent is hiding critical records from the situation or is even deceiving in the person that they virtually are. No depend quantity what form of deception is being deployed, most human beings agree that deception is dangerous and want to now not be completed.

Chapter 2: Brainwashing This chapter goes to interest on the process of brainwashing and all the components that encompass it. Through the media and the movies which can be visible, many human beings see brainwashing as an evil exercise that is finished by means of way of manner of mother and father which might be looking to corrupt, have an effect on, and to benefit strength. Some who really don't forget inside the energy of brainwashing trust that human beings all round them are looking for to manage their minds and their behavior.

For the maximum aspect, the way of brainwashing takes area in a much extra diffused way and does no longer comprise the sinister practices that maximum people partner with it. This financial disaster will bypass into loads extra detail about what brainwashing is and the manner it is able to have an impact on the venture's manner of questioning.

Chapter 9: What Is Brainwashing?

Brainwashing in this guidebook is probably discussed in phrases of its use in psychology. In this relation, brainwashing is known as a manner of idea reform thru social have an impact on. This sort of social impact is happening all in some unspecified time in the future of the day to all of us, no matter whether or not or now not they apprehend it or not. Social have an impact on is the collection of techniques which may be used so you can exchange one-of-a-type humans's behaviors, ideals, and attitudes. For example, compliance techniques which can be used within the workplace may additionally want to technically be taken into consideration a shape of brainwashing because of the reality they require you to act and assume a particular way whilst you're at the activity. Brainwashing can turn out to be more of a social trouble in its maximum severe form due to the fact the ones techniques artwork at changing the way someone thinks without the hassle consenting to it.

For brainwashing to art work effectively, the priority goes to want to go through a whole isolation and dependency due to its invasive affect on the problem. This is one of the reasons that maximum of the brainwashing instances which can be diagnosed about rise up in totalistic cults or prison camps. The brainwasher, or the agent, need as a way to gain whole control over their situation. This manner that they have got to govern the eating conduct, sleeping patterns, and enjoyable the opposite human goals of the undertaking and none of those moves can get up without the need of the agent. During this manner, the agent will paintings to systematically harm down the hassle's complete identification to basically make it no longer artwork right anymore. Once the identity is broken, the agent will art work to update it with the popular beliefs, attitudes, and behaviors.

The approach of brainwashing remains up for debate whether or not or no longer it'll paintings.

Most psychologists keep the beliefs that it's miles possible to brainwash a subject as long as the proper situations are gift. Even then, the whole technique is not as excessive as it's far supplied within the media. There also are specific definitions of brainwashing that make it more difficult to determine the effects of brainwashing at the priority. Some of these definitions require that there want to be a few form of hazard to the physical body of the task with a purpose to be taken into consideration brainwashing. If you comply with this definition, then even the practices completed through manner of many extremist cults have to not be considered proper brainwashing as no physical abuse takes location.

Other definitions of brainwashing will depend upon manage and coercion with out bodily pressure so that you can get the exchange in the beliefs of the subjects.
Either manner, experts be given as actual with that the impact of brainwashing, even below the proper conditions, is best a short term occurrence. They trust that the antique identification of the priority is not completely eliminated with the workout; as an alternative, it's far located into hiding and could return as quickly as the fashionable identity isn't always bolstered anymore.

Robert Jay Lifton came up with a few exciting mind on brainwashing within the 1950s after he studied prisoners of the Chinese and Korean War camps.
During his observations, he decided

that those prisoners underwent a multistep gadget to brainwashing.

This technique commenced with attacks on the enjoy of self with the prisoner after which ended with a meant trade in beliefs of the problem. There are 10 steps that Lifton defined for the brainwashing system within the subjects that he studied. These blanketed: 1. An assault on the identity of the scenario

2. Forcing guilt on the problem three. Forcing the task into self-betrayal
four.Reaching a breaking point
5.Offering the difficulty leniency in the occasion that they trade
6.Compulsion to confess 7. Channeling the guilt in the intended route
8.Releasing the concern of supposed guilt
9.Progressing to harmony
10.The final confession earlier than a rebirth
All of these degrees need to take area in a place this is in complete isolation.
This way that every one of the normal social references that the undertaking is used to coming in contact with are unavailable.

In addition, mind clouding strategies is probably employed to be able to expedite the method collectively with malnutrition and sleep deprivation. While this can not be authentic of all brainwashing instances, regularly there may be a presence of some type of bodily harm which contributes to the aim having hassle in questioning independently and drastically like they generally could in all likelihood.

Steps Used

While Lifton separated the steps of the brainwashing manner into 10 steps, contemporary-day psychologists installation it into three ranges as a way to higher recognize what is going on for the mission for the duration of this way. These 3

levels encompass the breaking down of the self, introducing the concept of salvation to the problem, and the rebuilding of the self of the mission.

Understanding every of those stages and the system that takes place with every of them can help you to understand what goes right now to the identification of the priority with this way.

Breaking Down of Self The first diploma of the brainwashing manner is the breaking down of the self. During this machine, the agent desires to split the vintage identity of the problem in order to reason them to experience greater inclined and open to the popular new identification. This step is vital that allows you to

keep at the manner. The agent isn't always going to be very a hit with their endeavors if the problem stays firmly set in their solve and their vintage identification. Breaking up this identity and making the person question the topics around them could make it easier to trade the identification within the later

steps. This is achieved via numerous steps which includes attack at the identity of the problem, brining on guilt, self-betrayal, and then achieving the breaking issue.

Assault on Identity

The attack at the character of the mission is largely the planned attack regarding the subjects' wholesome self-appreciation, or their self photograph or personality along their middle association of conviction. It makes

the scenario inquiry what their identity is through manner of spreading the word about them do not forget that each one that they have at any factor is off-base. The expert will make investments a whole lot of strength denying all that the challenge is. In detainee camps, as an instance, the expert will make statements like "You aren't protective opportunity," "You aren't someone," and "You aren't a warrior." The trouble can be below attacks like those usually for a clearly long time as much as months. This is completed to debilitate the topics truely in order that they grow to be muddled,

confounded, and depleted. Whenever the priority arrives at this shape of unique, their convictions will start to appear to be an entire lot much less sturdy and they may start to collect the things that they'll be knowledgeable

Guilt Once the situation has lengthy past through the assault on their person, they will input the section of culpability. The project is probably always informed that they are awful on the identical time as going thru this new individual emergency that has been welcomed on. This is executed to welcome a big feeling of duty at once to the state of affairs. The problem can be continually enduring an onslaught for any of the matters that they have completed, paying little thoughts to how big or little the demonstrations may be.

The scope of the assaults can fluctuate too; the issue might be censured for his or her conviction frameworks to the manner that they get dressed or perhaps because they eat too leisurely. Over the long run, the undertaking will start to revel in shame round them constantly and they'll revel in that the whole lot they are doing are off-base. This can assist with causing them to enjoy more helpless and susceptible to oblige the present day individual the expert wants to offer.

Self-betrayal Now that the difficulty has been persuaded to count on that they're awful and that each one in their sports are bothersome, the expert will attempt to strain the scenario to concede that they're terrible. Now, the difficulty is suffocating of their personal responsibility and feeling very disoriented.

Through the length of the intellectual attacks, the hazard of some exquisite actual mischief, or a combination of the two, the professional will certainly want to electricity the project to revile his antique identity.

This can include a huge collection of factors, as an example, getting the hassle to sentence their personal partners, companions, and circle of relatives who percent the equal perception

tool as them. While this cycle might also moreover require a extensive stretch of time to seem, while it does, the priority will feel like he deceived those who he feels committed to. This

will assemble the disgrace in addition to the deficiency of
character that the intention is now feeling, further isolating the character of the project.

Breaking Point

By this issue, the state of affairs is feeling extraordinarily separated and disoriented.

They is probably posing inquiries like Where am I? Who am I? Also, What would it not not now not be useful for me to do? The problem is in a person emergency now and is going via some profound shame. Since they've provided out the convictions as a whole and the people that he has generally recognized, the issue will undergo an disturbing breakdown.

In thoughts technological know-how, this honestly implies an assortment of high-quality side consequences that regularly reveal an large shape of assumed highbrow disturbances.
Some of the thing consequences can encompass favored confusion, profound unhappiness, and out of manage crying. The trouble might probably have the sensations of being actually lost alongside having a loose maintain on the actual global. When the

challenge arrives at this restrict, they'll have out of vicinity their wholesome self-awareness and the expert can basically do some thing they desire with them at this thing because the task has out of place how they may interpret what is taking vicinity spherical them and what their identification is. Additionally now, the expert will placed up the simplest of a type enticements which is probably crucial collectively to alternate over the undertaking in the direction of each one-of-a-kind conviction framework. The new framework might be installation in a way to offer salvation to the state of affairs from the hopelessness that they're feeling. Possibility of Salvation After the expert has been a hit at placing aside the self of the problem, the time has come to preserve on to the subsequent step.

This step includes offering the problem the threat of salvation supplied that they'll be capable of get a long way from their previous conviction framework and on 2d idea include the superior one this is being marketed. The challenge is authorized the possibility to understand what is around them, are informed that they might be extraordinary all yet again and they could sense advanced if they'll in reality follow the present day preferred route.

There are 4 stages which might be remembered for this phase of the programming machine; mercy, impulse to admission, directing of the responsibility and delivering of the guilt.

Leniency
Leniency is the "I assist you to" stage.

The trouble has been separated and forced to get some distance from the human beings and the convictions that they have got clutched for such limitless years. They had been informed that they're lousy and that all that they in fact do is off- base. The problem will revel in out of place and isolated on the earth, dishonorable by way of the use of any manner of the awful subjects that they have finished and brooding approximately what direction they may be capable to show.

When they arrive at this degree, the expert can provide them a sort of transport thru presenting to help them.

This will frequently be as a remedy from the maltreatment the project has precipitated or a few other little kindness.

For model, the expert can provide some extra meals or a beverage of water to the undertaking or perhaps take a couple of seconds to ask the assignment person inquiries concerning domestic and pals and family. In the project's gift popularity, those little considerate gestures will appear to be no joking depend, bringing about the hassle inclination a primary feeling of appreciation and help in the direction of the professional. Frequently those sentiments are manner tousled in evaluation with the contribution that has been made. In certain occurrences, the hassle could probable enjoy just like the professional has finished the demonstration of saving their life instead of clearly presenting a bit

assist. This twisting of sports works in the blessing of the professional as the project is presently going to collect ties of strength of mind with the professional in preference to matters of the beyond.

Compulsion to Confession

Once the professional has had the choice to gather the get hold of as true with of their challenge, they'll try to get an admission out of the approach.

This degree is regularly referred to as the "You can help your self." During this phase of the conditioning device, the problem starts offevolved offevolved to look the differences a few of the torment and culpability that they felt at some point of the person attack and the consolation that they'll be feeling from the surprising tolerance that is advertised. Assuming the conditioning machine is strong, the project might likely attempt and begin to feel a longing to reply a part of the generosity that has been proposed to them thru the usage of the professional. Whenever this happens, the professional will really need to introduce the possibility of confession as a potential way to freeing the difficulty from the aggravation and duty that they may be feeling. The problem will then be pushed thru a route of admitting the wrongs in well-known and sins that they've done within the past.

Of route, those wrongs and sins could be just like what they advocate for the brand new character this is being made. For example, assuming the difficulty is a captive, this improvement will allow them to confess the wrongs that they did with the aid of using safeguarding possibility or struggling with towards the device of the alternative u.S.. Regardless of whether or not these aren't in truth wrongs or sins, they warfare with the latest philosophy that the machine is typically correct as a result they want to be confessed.

Channeling of Guilt

Once the venture enters the diverting of culpability step, they were gift approach the attack in their self for a long time. When the problem arrives at this aspect within the conditioning device, they're capable of revel in the culpability and the shame that has been located on them, but it has essentially misplaced its

importance. They can't will let you recognise precisely what they've got fouled up to purpose them to feel as such; they actually apprehend that they are wrong.

The professional will really want to encompass the smooth canvas of the concern to explain why they're within the torment that they will be feeling. The professional will truly want to connect the feeling of responsibility that the hassle is feeling to

some difficulty they desire. Assuming the expert is attempting to supplant an affiliation of convictions, they'll take the vintage framework and convince the difficulty that the ones convictions are the issue are causing them to experience the obligation. Here the agreement some of the vintage convictions and the present day convictions are laid out; basically, the old conviction framework has been laid out to observe with the intellectual distress that the project has been feeling whilst the modern conviction framework has been laid out to relate with the capability to break out from that ache. The selection may be the subjects', however it's far quite clean to see that they could pick out the contemporary framework to begin feeling higher.

Releasing of Guilt
In this improvement, the hassle has come to apprehend that their antique characteristics and convictions are inflicting them torment. At this factor they may be wiped out and burnt out on feeling the culpability and disgrace that has been positioned on them for a long time. They begin to recognize that it isn't absolutely a few component that they have got carried out that motives them to feel as such; as an alternative, their convictions are inflicting the guilt.

The problem can feel some assist from the manner that there is a few element that they're capable of do approximately the guilt. They will likewise experience better for the reason that they currently have come to the comprehension that they will be not the terrible character, as an alternative it's miles humans that they've been close to and their conviction framework this is the real responsible birthday celebration this is causing the disquietude that is something that they may restore to turn out to be outstanding all all once more. The problem has decided that they have a technique for get out essentially thru manner of having a long way from a few unacceptable conviction framework that they have held and embracing the upgraded one that is being advertised. All that the mission want to do to deliver the obligation that they may be feeling is to sentence the establishments and people which is probably associated with the vintage conviction framework and then they'll be let out of the guilt.

The problem currently has some command over this degree. They will certainly need to recognize that the arrival of responsibility relies upon on them truely. All the state of affairs want to accomplish for this degree to be let out of the misleading terrific is to admit to any of the demonstrations they have got committed which might be associated with the antique conviction framework. When the general admission is completed, the concern ought to have completed the entire highbrow dismissal in their previous individual. The expert need to step in now to provide every different character to the situation and help them with reconstructing their person into the desired one.

Rebuilding of Self

By this progression, the state of affairs has lengthy beyond thru a ton of steps and personal strife. They have been positioned thru a problem that is supposed to strip them in their vintage individual, instructed that they may be horrible and ought to be fixed, and gradually arrive on the know-how that their conviction framework is the cause for their misleading extremely good and that it should be changed. When all of this has been reached, the challenge will want to determine out the manner to redesign their self, with the help of the agent.

This diploma permits the expert the opportunity to embed the thoughts of the new machine for the reason that state of affairs is a clean begin and pretty nerve-racking to determine out the manner to be and enjoy hundreds stepped forward. There are levels which can be visible sooner or later of this diploma along with amicability and the final admission preceding to starting over.

Harmony

The professional will contain this improvement to influence the situation that pursuing a alternate is their preference. They may additionally need to look the trouble that they have got the choice to select out what's wonderful and encourage a alternate as a manner to assist them to. The expert will then, at that component, gift the present day conviction framework and present it such that makes it the awesome or the exceptional choice. During this degree, the professional will prevent the maltreatment and on 2d concept strive supplying the difficulty intellectual quiet and actual solace. The cause inside the lower back of doing this is to adjust the vintage convictions to the aggravation and enduring at the equal time as at the identical time adjusting the present day day convictions to bliss and remedy.

This diploma is set up so the challenge is given the choice of which avenue to take, in spite of the truth that it definitely not does now not rely upon them. The hassle must make use of this diploma to pick out each the antique convictions and the cutting-edge convictions, honestly figuring out how they may experience until the prevent of their lives. By this problem, the hassle has previously long past thru the most commonplace way of reprimanding their vintage beliefs because of the tolerance and torture that they have got lengthy beyond thru. Along those strains, nearly definitely, they'll pursue the choice for the brand new affiliation of self notion to relieve their obligation. The new person that has been brought is attractive and solid thinking about that in reality no longer just like the vintage personality added at the breakdown in in advance than steps.

Utilizing cause and thinking about the thoughts-set that the situation is in, it is extra honest to peer that the principle man or woman that the problem will decide for their very very own inner serenity and protection is the ultra-modern one.

Final Confession and Starting Over

Even but the choice is honestly now not theirs thru any stretch of the creativeness, the expert has decisively worked the whole opportunity to guide the state of affairs to feeling like they've got the liberty of concept to select out the present day day character. Assuming the conditioning system is completed effectively, the concern will contemplate the ultra-modern-day picks and confirm that the high-quality one is to take inside the new individual. They have been tailored to preserve this attitude and of their new angle, the one appears OK. There can be no wonderful selections; choosing the cutting-edge person allows them to be feeling higher from the responsibility that they experience and prompts delight even as choosing the antique individual activates torment and culpability. On the off danger that for a few reason the difficulty denied the contemporary man or woman, there may be a backtracking within the whole brainwashing interplay and they is probably pressured to undergo everything once more to wind up with the proper outcomes.

During this segment of the cycle, the problem will stop that they will select out remarkable, and that means that they get to determine to go together with the new identification.

When the venture differences the desolation and torment in their vintage individual with the serenity that accompanies the present day, they will pick out the contemporary man or woman. This new character resembles a type of salvation. The component assists them with feeling masses better and no longer need to address duty and despondency any in addition. As this diploma finishes, the trouble will push aside their antique person and will undergo a course of vowing faithfulness to their new one, know-how that it'll paintings at making their life higher.

Many times, there are services and customs that occur at some stage in this ultimate stage. The transformation from the vintage individual to the latest man or woman isn't any joking don't forget because of the fact that tons investment has been carried out on the 2 factors. During those offerings, the problem is probably regularly taking place into the new nearby region and embraced with the brand new persona. For a few conditioning casualties there's the feeling of resurrection in the direction of this period.

You are authorized to include your new man or woman and are greeted
wholeheartedly into the modern-day close by region that is presently your very own. Rather than being disconnected and by myself, you've got were given severa new companions and community vicinity human beings on your side. Rather than feeling the culpability and ache

that has tormented you for a long term you will revel in satisfaction and tranquility with all that is spherical you. The new persona is currently yours and the conditioning trade is entire.

This cycle can get up over a time of severa months to even years.

Most people are set of their identity

and the convictions that they have got; it's far absurd to count on to trade all of this in handiest a couple of days besides if the character changed into at that issue able to exchange and that might make the indoctrinating techniques superfluous. Separation may likewise be essential in moderate of the truth that outside influences will preserve the problem from relying on the expert inside the path of this cycle.
This is the reason the greater a part of the programming instances take area in prison camps and one-of-a-kind separated examples; through a protracted way most of humans may not get the possibility of experiencing conditioning because of the manner that they may be normally encircled through the usage of human beings and innovation that could

frustrate the complete indoctrinating technique.

Once the man or woman is in disconnection, the way consumes a large chunk of the day because of the severa advances that ought to be taken to trade the necessities held by means of the character for a long time so they may encompass the state-of-the-art manner of lifestyles as their non-public at the same time as likewise feeling that the choice has for all time been theirs.

As want to be seen, there are numerous advances that want to be taken to undergo the indoctrinating gadget. Not a few element will take place just with the aid of on foot into any man or woman inside the metropolis and shopping for and promoting a couple of phrases. It requires the confinement and time to persuade the state of affairs that every one that they realise is off-base and that they may be a horrible character. It then, at that issue, progresses beforehand with searching for to power out an admission that the trouble is terrible and that they want to revoke the whole thing that they have carried out which might be awful because of their vintage individual. At prolonged remaining, the problem might be pushed in the direction of accepting that they may be able to improve in the event that they truely depart their antique thoughts and on second idea consist of the serenity and rightness that accompanies the brand new person that is introduced. These way have to manifest for the programming to be powerful and the modern-day personality to be positioned in location.

Brainwashing as Court Defense Throughout history, individuals had been making sure that they dedicated horrendous wrongs thinking about the truth that they have been brainwashed. It was a motive that many should assure looking forward to to save their very very personal lives or to tug off a mass murder or every other unspeakable atrocity. It need to try to be some factor as sincere as taking from someone else. Anything that the interest have grow to be, conditioning become a smooth protection as it made the duty of the bypass far from the charged and it changed into difficult to illustrate whether or not or no longer anybody have been indoctrinated or not.

Whether conditioning requests may be carried out as a safety inside the court in the long run relies upon on some speak. Numerous specialists enjoy that via using using allowing this protection into the court, the courts could

168

emerge as overpowered with bogus instances of programming and the assets for demonstrating or negating this defend may be beyond what the courts need to cope with. Regardless of this, there have been a few times added to court that could show the legitimacy of programming as a guard for violations dedicated.

The first illustration of this took place in 1976. Patty Hearst, the beneficiary to a big meting out fortune, done the protection of programming at the same time as she stood initial for a financial organization burglary. In the mid 1970s, Hearst became abducted with the useful aid of the SLA, the Symbionese Liberation Army, and wound up turning into a member of this agency.

During the preliminary, Hearst specific that she have been secured in a material cabinet for basically more than one days after she had been seized. While inside the garage room, Hearst expressed that she feared her existence, mistreated, tired, and changed into not sorted at the same time as people from the SLA barraged her with their philosophy in opposition to an industrialist u . S . A .. Inside the 2 months of her taking photos, Patty had modified her call whilst furthermore giving an articulation announcing that her family had been "pig-Hearsts" and in a while showed up on the safety tape of a monetary institution burglarizing it along facet the folks that had hijacked her.

In 1976, Patty Hearst stood initial for this monetary business enterprise robbery and modified into
safeguarded through F. Lee Bailey. In the defend, it turn out to be assured that Hearst were brainwashed with the useful useful resource of the SLA. This brainwashing had restrained Hearst to perpetrate a wrongdoing that she couldn't ever have completed below some other scenario. In the highbrow specific that she have become below with the programming, she could not differentiate amongst correct and awful and therefore ought not be considered as at fault for the financial institution theft. The courtroom docket disagreed with this exam and on 2nd idea tracked down her blameworthy and set her in prison for seven years. Only a couple of years after the reality, President Carter drove her sentence so she simply wound up burning through years altogether in jail.
Lee Boyd Malvo Case

Another splendid programming safety is the Lee Boyd Malvo case. This case applied the shield of craziness via conditioning and it wound up within the courts spherical 30 years after the Patty Hearst case. In 2002, Lee Boyd Malvo become being investigated for the hobby that he executed within the sharpshooter goes after that passed off round and in Washington D.C. Malvo, who modified into 17 at that component, and John Allen Muhammad, forty two, finished up killing 10 human beings and injuring 3 at a few degree in the killing binge. The protect that have become applied for this example became that the youngster Malvo have been conditioned through way of Muhammad so he might also perpetrate the violations. Very similar to in the Hearst case, the shield assured that Malvo couldn't have probable completed those wrongdoings inside the event that he had not been heavily encouraged with the aid of manner of way of Muhammad.

According to the muse tale utilized by the defend, Malvo were deserted via his mother at the island of Antigua inside the Caribbean at the same time as he have grow to be 15 years of age. Muhammad met the kid and carried him into the USA in 2001. Muhammad have become a army veteran at that point and attempted to fill the pinnacle of the immoderate schooler with desires of a race battle that become looming. Keeping that during thoughts, Malvo grow to be organized to be a professional marksman. As properly as imparting the ones plans to Malvo, Muhammad separated Malvo from others on the same time as being saturated with the antagonistic and kooky logo of Islam that Muhammad tracked with a excessive interest everyday and weight-reduction plan. All of that is famous to were a piece of the

conditioning tool on the youthful Malvo.

The defend contended that because of his time loved with Muhammad, Malvo have been indoctrinated and along these traces, he changed into not in form for telling what emerge as proper based totally on what emerge as incorrect.

Despite the endeavors of the safety, Malvo changed into considered as blameworthy and had a sentence of life in jail and now not the usage of a possibility of parole. In a one-of-a-type preliminary, Muhammad have become condemned to the loss of life penalty.

So some distance, it does not appear to be

brainwashing will acquire hundreds of floor as a sort of safety inside the court docket. Most importantly, it's miles excessively tough to illustrate that a litigant has been programmed anyhow. Then, it's miles a ways-fetched that all people has been conditioned and on 2nd idea the safety is in reality related to it as a manner to get a lighter sentence or the sports in their consumer forgiven. Also, numerous juries seem to keep in mind indoctrinating surely crazy.

Generally, this protect will maximum probably now not see loads of concord filling inside the court docket.

Common Tactics Used in Brainwashing Brainwashing isn't commonly quite plenty as extraordinary as what has been portrayed this sort of lengthy strategies in this element. The techniques portrayed are applied for "proper programming" and are seldom carried out to the concern.

There are numerous unique styles of conditioning that truely arise on an everyday basis.

They possibly might not attempt to make you absolutely surrender your antique individual for each other one, however they address organization to assist with moving your contemplations and mind on what is taking area around you. This element will 0 in on part of the strategies that are often achieved finally of the indoctrinating machine, paying little mind to whether or not or not it is legitimate conditioning or not.

Hypnosis-hypnosis, to be able to be examined in greater detail in the following phase, is a type of programming in superb situations. Spellbinding is

basically the enlistment of a excessive scenario of suggestibility. This kingdom is frequently masked meagerly as contemplation or unwinding. During the path of spellbinding, the expert can advocate topics to the priority in an effort to inspire them to act or reply in a superb way.

Many people are herbal with hypnosis from the degree indicates they've got visible. It is also everyday implemented as a way for enhancing fitness.

Peer Pressure-truely all people has a herbal need to have an area. This need to accompany a particular amassing, their own family, companions, and the nearby area. With the accomplice pressure method there is a concealment of the uncertainty that the task feels along doing away with their safety from groundbreaking mind with the aid of the use of using taking advantage of regions of power for this to have an area. Assuming that achieved nicely, the problem might be extra ready to evaluate new subjects, be loads tons much less bashful spherical new human beings, and might make some less hard reminiscences making new friends.

Love Bombing — the feeling of family is number one regions of energy for in particular people. This is the gathering which you have been certainly
introduced to and which you have as an extended manner as everyone is aware of been round to your complete life. They recognize you better than truely anybody and the humans who've exceeded up this form of courting might observe that they may be feeling on my own and unwanted. With adoration bombarding, the expert
ought to make a experience of the circle of relatives via the utilization of close to domestic maintaining, feeling and through sharing and actual contact. This allows the expert and the hassle to bond in a familial manner, making it

easier to exchange the antique character for the modern one.

Rejecting Old Values — as referenced absolutely previous in this section, the professional is attempting to steer the hassle to censure the entirety of their personal traits. This cycle is accelerated through the course of terrorizing, actual threat, and precise approach. Toward the give up, the hassle will
condemn the traits and convictions that they once held close and will begin to renowned the modern-day way of lifestyles this is introduced to them through the agent.

Confusing Doctrine — on this method, there can be a consolation to aimlessly widely known the new man or woman even as dismissing one in every of a type motive that the hassle will have. To do this, the expert will go through a complicated association of talks approximately a law that allows you to be endless.
The mission will parent out the way to aimlessly take delivery of as real with what the professional is speakme about via this interaction, whether or no longer it is about the convention or about the brand new character that is being fashioned.

Metacommunication — this technique is completed at the same time as the professional attempts to embed diffused turns on into the mind of the priority. This is probably finished at the same time as the expert focuses on particular words or expressions that are essential to the modern individual. These expressions and watchwords can be
embedded into confounding long talks that the venture can be pressured to sit down down through.

No Privacy — privacy is an honor that many subjects will lose till they've got changed over to the latest man or woman that

is gave to them. In addition to the fact that that is eliminated as a way to make the culpability and unsoundness greater evident to the assignment, but it furthermore gets rid of the capability the problem wishes to continuously check the matters that they are being informed. Assuming the priority is permitted to have protection, they have got possibility and strength to secretly consider the statistics they may be given and might find out that it's far faux or won't maintain as a great deal as what they as of now take delivery of. Removing this protection means that the expert or specialists are continuously close to and the task is constantly being directed to the brand new identification.

Disinhibition — in the course of this approach, the issue is cautioned via the professional to present sincere dutifulness. This makes it

less complex for the professional to noticeably impact the mind of the hassle.

Unbending Rules — the includes a decision which is probably set up with the resource of the expert are regularly extreme and won't ever be changed. These necessities are presupposed to make it hard for the trouble to assume and test up on their personal; as an alternative, they'll make investments their energy doing the exact element they may be informed to do through the professional. There are a large form of makes a choice that would squeeze into this beauty, for example, the pointers a great way to be decided for the

confusion and relapse approach the whole thing the manner to how the trouble is permitted to make use of meds, take washroom breaks, and devour suppers. These suggestions are set up to virtually control the scenario at some degree within the conditioning technique.

Verbal Abuse — verbal misuse is one of the techniques that is applied at some stage in the preserving aside diploma. Frequently the trouble becomes desensitized
at the same time as they'll be barraged with risky and foul language constantly. On occasion, actual maltreatment might also additionally decorate or supplant verbal abuse.

Sleep Deprivation — at the equal time as an individual isn't getting how plenty rest that they require they'll often come to be powerless and at a loss for words. This can help with putting in place the wonderful weather that the expert is attempting to find in the end of the retaining apart and admission stages of the conditioning system.
Likewise, generally the difficulty can be required to do delayed bodily and highbrow physical games on pinnacle of the lacking snooze request to rush the cycle even more.

Dress Codes — implementing a apparel law further gets rid of any place of understanding that the hassle may also additionally have in addition to the choice they're applied to of selecting their non-public garments. Frequently at a few degree in the indoctrinating gadget, the assignment can be requested to area at the apparel regulation held through the use of the the rest of the organization.

Chanting — the professional will try to take out any non-clique thoughts that is probably available in the thoughts of the concern.

One method for undertaking this is thru reciting or reiteration of the expressions which can be used by the individuals who follow the brand new identification.

Confession — confession is profoundly energized in the folks who are transforming from their antique character to the ultra-modern character. During this interplay, the challenge will destruct their very very own singular self image via the use of admitting each one in each of their inner maximum sensations of uncertainty and person shortcomings to the expert. When they might relinquish these objects, the presentation of the modern day character can arise.

Financial Commitment — in some instances, there may be financial
commitments which ought to be met. This can assist the expert in some techniques.

First, the financial responsibility permits an extended reliance of the project on the gathering in moderate of the fact that the assignment might be severing ties to their beyond. They will supply numerous resources, whether or no longer it's miles their car, residence, coins, or a few different economic self-control in the expectations that they will simply want to move past their shame and responsibility. Presently they will be monetarily joined to the modern-day day identity.

In boom, the expert will truly want to utilize the ones economic commitments to assist their very own desires.

Pointing the Finger — while you can blame every unique character, you'll revel in a sense of honesty. This is your approach to telling the location that you are first rate essentially by using manner of bringing up part of the weaknesses which is probably going on within the international. The professional may want to probably carry up the whole thing of the killing, bigotry, and voracity which can be on the planet previous to differentiating it to the benefit of the modern day individual that the trouble is being pushed to.

Isolation — in case you are restrained from all that is round you, it turns into difficult to pay attention outside mind that might change your thoughts. This is what the professional will take a stab at because of the truth they do now not keep in mind all of their paintings must disappear. The oldsters which can be being conditioned may be remoted from society, partners, own family, and a few thing exceptional intention references that might appreciably regulate their method of questioning.

Controlled Approval — the expert will artwork to keep up with the confusion and weak factor of the scenario for the duration of the keeping apart time body.
One approach for doing this is thru controlled endorsement. The professional will as an alternative rebuff and prize comparative sports, making it tough for the task to understand what is accurate and what is inaccurate.

Change of Diet — converting how lots meals the difficulty is authorized to eat is one greater method used to make bewilderment at the equal time as increasing the powerlessness of the scenario to close to domestic pleasure. At the point even as the expert decisively diminishes how an entire lot food that the task is authorized to eat, they are denying the situation's sensory device of the vitamins which might be critical to thrive.

Adding medicinal pills to the combo might also likewise be brought into this magnificence.

Games — video video games are proper right here and there utilized to instigate extra reliance on the gathering. Games may be furnished and the big majority of them ought to have honestly dark thoughts that the problem may not understand. In sure occurrences, the scenario won't be knowledgeable the necessities and that they should type them out or the thoughts will constantly change. This technique allows the expert to accumulate manage.

No Questions — inside the route of the programming gadget, the difficulty isn't legal to are searching out clarification on urgent troubles. Questions increase man or woman reasoning and this is risky to the programming exercise.

When no inquiries are accepted, it assists the expert with attaining an automated acknowledgment from the challenge to the modern identity.

Guilt — the situation has been knowledgeable that they are lousy and that each one that they do is horrible. Responsibility is an everyday technique that is utilized by the expert to make the difficulty inquiry their convictions and what is taking area spherical them. The wrongdoings of the problem's preceding manner of existence can be misrepresented to reap the culpability and help the want of salvation within the challenge.